Preserving Electronic
Evidence for Trial

Preserving Electronic Evidence for Trial

A Team Approach to the Litigation Hold, Data Collection, and Evidence Preservation

Ann D. Zeigler

Ernesto F. Rojas

ELSEVIER

AMSTERDAM • BOSTON • HEIDELBERG • LONDON
NEW YORK • OXFORD • PARIS • SAN DIEGO
SAN FRANCISCO • SINGAPORE • SYDNEY • TOKYO
Syngress is an imprint of Elsevier

SYNGRESS.

Syngress is an imprint of Elsevier
50 Hampshire Street, 5th Floor, Cambridge, MA 02139, USA

Notices
Knowledge and best practice in this field are constantly changing. As new research and experience broaden our understanding, changes in research methods, professional practices, or technical procedures may become necessary.

Practitioners and researchers must always rely on their own experience and knowledge in evaluating and using any information, methods, or techniques described herein. In using such information or methods they should be mindful of their own safety and the safety of others, including parties for whom they have a professional responsibility.

To the fullest extent of the law, neither the Publisher nor the authors, contributors, or editors, assume any liability for any injury and/or damage to persons or property as a matter of products liability, negligence or otherwise, or from any use or operation of any methods, products, instructions, or ideas contained in the material herein.

British Library Cataloguing-in-Publication Data
A catalogue record for this book is available from the British Library

Library of Congress Cataloging-in-Publication Data
A catalog record for this book is available from the Library of Congress

ISBN: 978-0-12-809335-1

For information on all Syngress publications
visit our website at http://store.elsevier.com/Syngress

Typeset by Thomson Digital

Dedication

To Ernesto Francisco Rojas, my coauthor, who died unexpectedly in October 2014, two days after sending me the first draft of his half of this book, for his friendship and for his encouragement in this adventure, and to our spouses, Ann's favorite photographer-poet Paul Zeigler, and Ernesto's beloved Raisa.

Special thanks to Ernesto's colleague, Ross A. Leo, FABCHS, CISSP, HCISPP, CHS-IV, ABCP, Associate Director, Professional Training & Development, University of Houston-Clear Lake, CyberSecurity Institute (http://www.uhcl.edu/CyberSecurityInstitute) for his generosity in providing a technical review of the completed manuscript.

Dedication

Contents

Author Biographies

Ernesto F. Rojas, CISSP, CCFP, DFCP (1950–2014)

Associate Director (Services), Cyber-Security Institute, University of Houston-Clear Lake, 2014
Certified Information Systems Security Professional (CISSP), 2013–14
American Academy of Forensic Sciences, 2012–14
Chair, Accreditation Committee, Digital Forensics Certification Board, 2011–12
Digital Forensics Certified Practitioner (DFCP), 2010–14
Association of Certified Fraud Examiners, 2009–11
Licensed Private Investigator (Texas), 2007–14
Licensed Private Security Consultant (Texas), 2007–11
Diplomate, American College of Forensic Examiners, 2006–14
President/CEO, Forensic & Security Services Inc., 2005–14
Certified Cyber Forensics Professional, (ISC)^2 (CCFP), 2003–14
Numerous professional publications and presentations
MBA, Pepperdine University, 1981
BS, Mechanical Engineering, Loyola University, 1972
BS, Accounting, Loyola University 1971

Ann D. Zeigler, MFA, JD

Who's Who in America (Marquis) 2003–15
Sisters in Crime, Croak & Dagger (Albuquerque) Chapter, vice president 2015
Mystery Writers of America, Southwest Chapter (Houston), program chair 2008–13
FBI (Houston) Citizens' Academy, 2009 (corp. secretary/director 2009–12)
Volunteer, Houston Police Dept., Juvenile Sex Crimes Unit, 2008–13
Houston Police Dept. Citizens' Academy, 2008
The Houston Lawyer editorial board 1999–2011, Editor in Chief 2009–10
Texas Supreme Court Committee on the Unauthorized Practice of Law, Attorney-Investigator (Dist. 4), 2004–13

Private practice, Houston 1984–2012
Admitted to Practice before the Texas Supreme Court (1984), US Fifth Circuit
Court of Appeals, United States District Courts for the Northern, Southern,
Eastern & Western Districts of Texas
Executive Editor, Houston Journal of International Law, 1983–84
JD, University of Houston, 1984
MFA Creative Writing, University of Montana, 1975
BA Magna Cum Laude, Fort Wright College, 1969

Introduction

We begin by telling you what this book is not intended to be. It is not an academic textbook. It is not an academic analysis of anything. It is not a technical training guide for either lawyers or computer forensics personnel.

This book is a handbook for businesses, to be used in forming and training an evidence-preservation and litigation-support team. This book will be useful to law students and IT/forensics students in understanding the complexities of evidence identification and preservation. But those advanced students are not our target audience.

We have a single goal—to keep businesses from inadvertently destroying evidence. The path to that goal is formation of a team whose members understand each other's technical languages and thereby avoid mishandling the contents of electronic systems and devices. We will be talking about practical steps to take as well as wider perspectives in evidence preservation. Every team member will learn to understand the languages spoken by the other team members before anyone needs to take action.

The team will be ready at the moment something happens that makes a future lawsuit (or regulatory action) likely. This is the moment the team will execute the litigation hold (about which you will learn) by effectively identifying, collecting, preserving, analyzing, and producing all appropriate electronic evidence.

In the face of a lawsuit, the entire team needs to understand the advice from lawyers as well as advice from computer forensics experts and IT personnel. The lawyers and forensics consultants will have specific advice for management about preserving the electronic evidence related to the dispute. Their joint task, before giving that advice, is to confirm to each other that they are all saying the same thing, regardless of technical terms, when they communicate within the team, and when the team communicates to the decision-makers.

We are here to give your team the wider picture about electronic evidence so you can all understand and cooperate effectively in preserving electronic evidence. We want every team member to understand the two parts of this concept: "electronic" and "evidence." And, more importantly, we want all of your team members to understand each other. The object—no surprises.

This book is intended to be used in enterprise education—building an effective team of highly-skilled people with different professional vocabularies, then making sure they are all communicating with each other. We will be talking about how you can translate critical concepts in those specialized vocabularies, and how to develop a team that is fluent in legal and technical vocabularies. This is the team that will preserve ("hold") all electronically stored information (metadata as well as content) as soon as there is some likelihood of future litigation (the "triggering event").

We will concentrate on civil litigation, where one party sues another. Where appropriate we will also point out issues of particular concern in regulatory compliance and investigations, and in criminal cases such as fraud and cyber crime where your business is a target or victim.

Information is information. Evidence, on the other hand, can be useful information for resolving a dispute, or completely worthless, depending on its reliability—including how it was handled. Lack of communication among team members using different specialized vocabularies is a shortcut to a bad outcome in a legal dispute. It is nearly as disastrous as having no team at all. Consider for a moment the memo from the trial lawyers to in-house counsel, the CEO, and CFO, asking for a $2.8 million check payable to the other side under a sanctions order, as one of the punishments for handing over incomplete electronic evidence and destroying the rest—not the memo you want your initials on. If you had a plan and a team in place before the dispute even arose, and your team members all understood each other, this would not be one of your nightmares.

In Chapter 1, we will consider basic technological and legal vocabulary everyone should learn now rather than in the middle of litigation. This includes in-house counsel and other management personnel, IT managers, forensic consultants, and outside litigation counsel. All these individuals must be on the same page about technology before litigation becomes likely, to effectively identify and preserve electronic evidence. Our focus is on active, accurate communication within the team, before the lawsuit as well as during the discovery process, settlement evaluation, and trial. We will give you a short review of the stages of civil lawsuits, focusing on the Federal Rules of Civil Procedure and how to use them to your advantage in managing electronic evidence issues at each stage.

Our goal is for your evidence team to have properly handled your electronically-stored information ("ESI") before it is handed over to your opponent, preserving its value as evidence, and avoiding not just pitfalls but absolute disaster. We will also discuss the other side of the preservation coin, understanding what you want from your opponent so you can ask for it effectively. In Chapter 2, we will look briefly at some legendary failures of preservation, such as the *Zubulake* and *Pension Committee* cases, and give you straight information about straight thinking where electronic information management is concerned. We will focus on the 2015 amendments to the Federal Rules, especially 34 and 37, and what drove the federal judiciary to "fix" their 2006 "fix" to the electronic evidence hold procedure.

The effective route to using these legal and nonlegal concepts to your advantage in litigation is team communication—using the right people to manage the process of electronic data preservation and production, and getting the process launched long before anyone is standing in a courtroom. But how do you gather and manage the team? In Chapter 3, we will analyze the strengths of various business personnel, and show you how to find the right skills in your organization.

Chapter 4 begins the heart of this book. In this chapter and Chapters 5 and 6, a computer forensics consultant leads you through the critical information your team needs at the moment you will only recognize in hind-sight, the triggering event. When you find out after the fact that an incident has occurred, your team will already know the answers to the important electronic evidence questions: what is it, and where is it.

In Chapter 7, we will consider the concept of data management and how to use it to your advantage. We will also consider why data mapping is not only a cost-saving measure, but a necessary business practice. It will be a critical tool in responding to litigation as well as in preventing data breaches. If you don't know where your data resides and why, you cannot be sure you have "everything" about a dispute, and if your network is hacked or otherwise compromised that "everything" is safe from bad actors.

Chapter 8 takes on the application of data policies and procedures in the litigation hold process. It is a series of questions your team must be able to answer cooperatively, addressing the structure of your organization and the related structure of your data systems.

In Chapter 9, we touch on the emerging area of Cloud Computing and other complex environments, and why the rules for physical systems go wrong when assumptions about other systems are inappropriately applied to the Cloud and/or these environments. We will also discuss a legal concept of "possession, custody, or control" that will be critical to the team's actions in activating the litigation hold.

In Chapter 10, we will lead you through the process from the triggering event onward, showing you how your Team members will reinforce each other's skills to put you in the best position to use the electronic evidence you hold, how to effectively obtain the opponent's electronic evidence, and how to evaluate it when it is produced to you.

In Chapter 11, we will discuss in detail the effective as well as disastrously ineffective use of the Federal Rule 26 "meet and confer" (and similar state-law requirements) early in litigation. This opportunity to control electronic evidence production is often fluffed or ignored by attorneys. We will show you how it can be a defining moment for control of electronic evidence discovery, setting the stage for early and beneficial dispute resolution, and why it is critical for every member of the Team to understand the 2015 revisions to the Federal Rules of Civil Procedure.

We conclude in Chapter 12 with a brief overview of international issues, which can affect the team's approach to both holding and obtaining electronic evidence. This will include a brief consideration of countries following the common law legal tradition and countries following the civil law tradition, and various region-wide legal regimes related to electronic privacy and cross-border jurisdictional problems. We will also discuss the work of several international working groups whose aim is to make this complex situation workable as international business grows.

The final element of this handbook is the Resource Appendix—a selected list of our favorite sources of legal and technical updates.

We hope this book will serve as a guide to efficient collection, preservation, and analysis of electronic data as evidence in dispute resolution, by effective use of the entire Team.

The Authors

CHAPTER 1

Your Critical Task: Learn Another Language

A COMPUTER FORENSICS EXPERT LOOKS AT LEGALESE

- Electronic evidence?
- ESI?
- Spoliation?
- Federal Rules?
- Hold?
- Triggering event?
- Sedona Conference?
- 26? 34? 37(e)?
- Accurate preservation?

CONTENTS

When in the 1990s (last century) I, as a computer forensics expert, began to hear terms like these, I was confused and bothered, especially because these terms were used by lawyers or by people who worked with and talked to lawyers. I was talking to these people all the time, but I did not understand them.

This confusing scenario drove me to become familiar with the legal terms and what they meant. By the time the Federal Rules of Civil Procedure and similar state laws were revised in 2006 to specifically address my domain, electronic information, I realized that the translation business needed to be a two-way street. Forensics consultants and information technology/cyber-security personnel need to understand lawyers. Lawyers need to understand "that IT guy." Moreover, management needs a basic understanding of both.

In the world of computer technology, we use terms that are highly descriptive and that specify the object being discussed. For example, "corrupted data" means the data—electronic information—does not represent the original intended content any longer. "Spoliation" is a legal term that represents the same thing—the value of the electronic data no longer represents the original intended content.

This book is about how these and other different sets of terms reflect best (and worst) practices in handling electronic data as evidence in a legal dispute. The same concepts apply whether the dispute is about internal corporate misconduct, a contract dispute, or external fraud, in a mid-size company or a complex regulated industry, as either plaintiff or defendant. The company as crime victim must act in a different context from the company as a party to a civil trial. The same is true when the company is the target of a regulatory investigation—same concepts, different context.

Regardless of the context, the preservation of electronic information is the same. Moreover, the need for the legal and forensic experts to take action is equally critical in all contexts, whether as plaintiff or defendant, victim, target, or innocent bystander-witness.

THE CIVIL LAWSUIT—A PRETRIAL TOUR, WITH VOCABULARY

Speaking of plaintiffs and defendants, let us start with a legal vocabulary lesson, by working through the pretrial stages of a civil lawsuit in federal district court in which one party sues another. We will talk about business lawsuits here, although the process is the same when the parties are individuals.

Throughout this book, we will be talking about the Federal Rules of Civil Procedure, which we will refer to as the "Rules." There are Federal Rules of Evidence, Federal Rules of Criminal Procedure, and Federal Rules of Bankruptcy Procedure, which contain specific provisions about electronic evidence. We will not be discussing them. The experts know where to find them, and how to wrap them into the concepts we are working with here. We promise to stay away from the deep end of the conceptual pool.

We are working with the Federal Rules for ease of reference. Many states have mirrored their rules on these, so that you do not need to be in US District Court to use the concepts. A team is a team in any lawsuit.

So, without further ado, the lawsuit.

The Litigation Process, Word by Word

Anyone, whether an individual or a business, is in legalese a party. A party is the same as a person. (A corporation is a legal "person," although a general partnership is not a separate person but a group of individuals.)

The party complaining about the actions of another party is the plaintiff.

The party defending against the complaint is the defendant. There can be multiple plaintiffs and/or defendants.

The defendant can complain in return about the plaintiff, which is a counterclaim.

The defendant can also complain about the actions of someone else entirely, which is a third-party action. This is in the nature of the "he made me do it" defense.

The document filed (electronically, of course) in federal court by the plaintiff to begin a lawsuit is the complaint. In many state courts, this document is called the petition. The complaint must include enough factual details that the defendant and the judge can understand exactly what happened and why the plaintiff is entitled to win the lawsuit. It must, in the words of the Rules, be a "short and plain statement of facts" (Rule 1) showing that the plaintiff has been economically damaged and that the law requires the defendant to pay for that economic loss. (With your permission, we will skip the parts about emotional damages, damage to reputation, and other complications.)

To get into federal court, rather than state court, the complaint must also show proper "jurisdiction"—that the parties are in the right court. This could be a question of whether the plaintiff and defendant have their corporate control centers in different states and one of them does business across state lines, or that a federal law controls the dispute, such as copyright, trademark or patent disputes, or that one party is operating in bankruptcy, maritime/shipping/fisheries disputes, and of course, international disputes.

In the absence of one of the specific reasons to be in federal court, the case is dismissed (tossed out entirely without regard to the facts). Or it may be "removed" to state court, or vice-versa, if the dispute is filed in state court but belongs in federal court.

The plaintiff must properly serve (deliver) a copy of the complaint by the method provided in the Rules to the individual who is designated under the Rules to receive lawsuit papers for the defendant. The complaint must be accompanied by the summons, a document issued by the court that gives the deadline for the defendant to respond and the electronic or physical addresses to which the answer must be sent.

The defendant either files an answer (in some state courts, a response) by the deadline, or files a pre-answer objection to some major deficiency in the complaint—wrong defendant, wrong court, wrong kind of service, too late, or (most popular of all) "failure to state a claim upon which relief can be granted" (Rule 12(b)(6)). If the judge finds any of these preliminary objections to be valid, the lawsuit stops right there by dismissal. If the judge finds that the preliminary objections are not accurate, or if the problem can be solved by amending the complaint, then the plaintiff gets another try and the defendant's deadline to answer gets reset.

If the defendant fails to file an answer to the complaint by the deadline, the plaintiff gets a default judgment, after proving the summons and complaint were served to the proper address, using the proper procedure, and the proper amount of time has passed. The default judgment gives the plaintiff whatever the complaint asked for, without a trial or any further consideration by the court. In litigation between companies with experienced lawyers, this outcome is profoundly unlikely.

A hearing is a meeting in the courtroom between the lawyers for the parties and the judge, with the exact content of each person's statements taken down electronically by a court reporter for the record. The usual purpose of a hearing is for the lawyers to offer sworn statements by witnesses (witness testimony, including documents) to support a motion (a written request for the judge to order something). Ignoring a judge's order is contempt of court.

When both the complaint and answer are on file, the judge sets the date for the initial status hearing. The only purpose of the initial status hearing is to issue the pretrial order, setting the deadlines and limits for discovery.

Discovery is the pretrial process of obtaining the other side's evidence (witnesses and documents) and responding to requests for your evidence. Discovery takes many forms—interrogatories (written questions to be answered under oath), depositions (oral questioning of witnesses under oath, recorded by a licensed court reporter), requests for production (written requests for specific kinds of documents or physical objects), requests for admissions (specific factual statements to be admitted or denied under oath). Each of the forms of discovery has its own Rule, and each can inspire its own forms of gamesmanship.

Before that initial status hearing, and before discovery can begin, the attorneys for the two sides are required to cooperate for two specific purposes (Rule 26). First, each side must give certain basic information to the other. The required disclosures include (1) the names and contact information of individuals who are likely to have information about the dispute; (2) copies of "all documents, electronically stored information (ESI), and tangible things" which support the party's position, or lists of the names and locations of those forms of information; (3) each side's calculation of its financial damage, with copies of or access to any documentation supporting the calculation; and (4) information about any insurance or other indemnity agreement that might be available to pay the judgment if the plaintiff wins (Rule 26(a)).

The second requirement of Rule 26 that concerns us, the "meet and confer," is one we will discuss in depth later. This is the meeting of the attorneys at the very beginning of the lawsuit for the specific purpose of jointly planning for discovery. The parties' lawyers must appear at the initial status hearing before the judge with a written joint plan containing the specifics of their agreement about discovery. The court will enter that agreement as an order and enforce it as one (Rule 26(f)).

Throughout the remaining pretrial process, when one of the parties wants the judge to do something (or, more likely, make the other side do something), the written request is a "motion" stating what the party wants and why it is entitled to have an order for that. An order is only about that limited topic. At the end of the lawsuit, the court's final word on the subject (perhaps including a jury verdict) is a judgment, by which the court ends the lawsuit.

From that initial scheduling hearing until the final pretrial hearing to set the trial schedule, everything that happens is about discovery. It is about cooperation, or not. It is about preserving evidence, or not. It is about providing electronic evidence in an accessible format, or not. It is about finding out the actual facts on which a judgment can reliably rest or an appropriate settlement be negotiated, or not.

THE REAL FIRST STEP—THE TRIGGERING EVENT

But before any of these pretrial steps set out in detail in the Rules, there is one critical step that is not specifically described there, because it occurs before the lawsuit begins. That step is the critical one, the one this book is about.

The step is recognizing in very prompt fashion the moment when something bad happens and litigation becomes likely. The incident is the "triggering event." That event pulls the "hold" trigger, the duty to immediately send out a notice throughout your organization to hold (preserve) all information, everywhere, that might relate to the triggering event.

ESI IN THE RULES, OR HOW TO AGGRAVATE THE JUDGE

For our purpose, and for many companies, that in-house litigation-hold notice to save all the information concerns, basically, ESI. Some of the saved information will turn out to be nothing legally significant. Some of it will be actual courtroom evidence. All of it will need immediate preservation, at least for the short term. That preservation must be carried out by people who know what they want to find and use, plus people who know how to do preservation correctly ("forensically defensible preservation"), plus people who know all the places it can be found.

From before the beginning of computer use in business, up until 2006, the word "document" in the Rules meant, mostly, paper because what was actually available was, mostly, paper.

Slowly technology shifted and grew until most information was both created and kept, as it is now, in electronic formats—in many different kinds of electronic storage, in many different formats, some of which were only marginally capable of being retrieved in any understandable form.

Predictably, as technology changed and developed lawyers took the opportunity to object to producing the information from electronic storage. Parties in lawsuits did not get ESI documents from the opposing party because they failed to ask for the ESI in the precise electronic format it was kept in, even though they could not possibly know what format it was kept in. The hide-the-evidence game rollicked on. Motions to compel production of documents became the standard, not the exception, in trial preparation. Judges were spending more time dealing with technology squabbles among the lawyers than they spent trying cases. ESI became the elephant in the room of civil litigation.

An aggravated federal judiciary can be an inspired federal judiciary. In 2006, the US Supreme Court and Congress approved amendments to the Rules related to the management and inclusion of electronic evidence in federal court cases. A majority of states adopted either the 2006 Federal Rules amendments or a variation of them. The federal amendments came from the Rules Advisory Committee of the Federal Judicial Conference, the organization of all federal judges. The Rules Advisory Committee had spent many months considering how to be clear that "all" evidence includes "all" electronically stored evidence.

By 2010, it was obvious to federal judges throughout the country that electronic evidence had again become a serious venue for game playing, time wasting, and fee inflation. It had become another chance for brinksmanship, for aggressive lawyers to "litigate the other guy into the ground." State court judges were finding the same thing. Judges everywhere were muttering, or even saying aloud, "Why not just deal with the electronic evidence the same way you deal with the paper evidence? What don't you understand about 'all'?"

As you can easily deduce, when the judicial aggravation level gets that high, amendments follow. The latest round of amendments to the discovery Rules became effective on December 1, 2015. They are focused on the effective preservation, identification, and exchange of electronic evidence, with new clarity about proportionality—a concept, we will revisit at length.

KEEPING IT IN PROPORTION, ROUND 1: TRAINING

In my experience as a computer forensic consultant, there is now a two-tier ranking system for implementing the electronic evidence preservation process as part of the day-to-day work of handling litigation.

In the first tier, you have the companies such as Exxon, Wal-Mart, GE, Boeing, and other Fortune-listed mega-companies. These companies have fully staffed departments dedicated to distributing litigation-hold notifications, identifying custodians and systems, collecting evidence, and supporting litigation counsel over the entire course of the litigation hold, collecting the electronic evidence to support their side of a legal dispute.

The second tier, outside of those well-prepared mega-entities, consists of thousands of business organizations ill-equipped to implement the litigation hold. These companies' management do not understand in a practical way how the hold can be carried out by their employees, much less how those employees can adequately collect the information necessary to support the organization's side of the legal dispute.

This situation has become common, and many people in the litigation support field as well as business management ask people like us how to address the problems this situation raises. My unscientific observations of the problems and the disparities between the two tiers of litigants is focused on how litigation holds are analyzed and implemented.

There appear to be three principal causes for ineffective response to the litigation hold requirements of analysis and implementation: (1) insufficient focus on available human resources, (2) lack of technical education and training, and (3) inadequate or improper implementation of the electronic information hold. These are aggravated by failures of accurate communication between management and legal counsel. I am not necessarily addressing microbusinesses and home-based businesses. I am referring to mid-sized companies with several thousand employees. Preparing an organization for upcoming litigation is a matter of training, education, and preparation of everyone within the organization. This is a multidisciplinary effort, and it requires knowledge of multiple areas of the business to successfully achieve the goal—an efficient litigation hold, resulting in collection and preservation of appropriate ESI, which may be evidence for the case.

Shortly after the Federal Rules amendments were published in 2006, I presented a paper concerning the concept of the legal-incident response team, which is comprised of representatives from the legal department, litigation counsel, IT and records management professionals, and appropriate members of management. This team could in short order dissect the legal issues and focus the company's effort into identifying and collecting specific data in response to the specific challenge at hand.

Today very few medium-sized companies have implemented such a team process. Those Fortune 500 companies I mentioned earlier have all created teams that do this every day and can accomplish their task with minimal disruption to business operations. Not so for the average mid-sized company. For example, I have seen IT departments try to hold all the data created by numerous employees for the entire length of the litigation, creating a storage crisis.

Alternatively, information is not collected from process equipment that generates critical readings of what is occurring at the time of an incident, so that important evidence is overwritten every few days.

What can the organization that lacks this teamwork capability do? In the situation where there is no team in place, litigation counsel needs to consider creating one on the fly after litigation has started, by bringing in an outside expert who is experienced in both computer forensics and litigation, to serve as the point of guidance for the organization. This expert can advise on how to implement the litigation hold to save the remaining electronic evidence, educate employees, identify data repositories, understand and communicate how the information systems operate and their current settings, and develop a collection plan that has a low level of disruption to the organization.

The panic-attack response requires a specialist who can speak to both in-house and outside litigation counsel, to advise them of the conditions of the information systems prior to the Rule 26(f) meeting, and to support counsel's negotiations with opposing counsel. The expert must also work with management, assisting those individuals to understand the formal and informal workings of the organization about electronic information, as well as working with the IT personnel, to help management understand the systems operating within the company. This is the basis for developing a plan to efficiently collect the relevant evidence for the case.

Ignoring these management issues is a failure to understand the negative effects of later claims of spoliation, accusations of concealment of missed critical evidence, unpleasant surprises in the courtroom, and other unfavorable events that can come to roost at your company's feet, and yours as litigator or IT manager.

KEEPING IT IN PROPORTION, ROUND 2: THE PRICE OF COMPLIANCE, OR NOT

During the four years the Rules Advisory Committee spent preparing the 2015 Rules amendments, it held several national conferences, primarily a major conference at Duke University School of Law. The Duke Conference was followed by a long series of public meetings between the committee members and lawyers all around the country.

According to the Committee Notes, which are part of the amendments, many of the meetings featured corporate counsel complaining bitterly that actually holding "all" ESI was sending their companies to economic ruin because of the hideous expense of segregated electronic storage. At each of the meetings, the Committee requested those corporate lawyers to provide some actual dollars-and-cents facts about the costs of electronic storage. The Committee Notes point out rather sharply that no one actually provided any information about storage costs. That would presumably be a function of the enormous drop in electronic storage costs as technology has progressed in that area, such that huge data storage has become extremely cheap.

As a result of the expressions of distress by corporate counsel, however, the Committee took a renewed look at the wording of Rule 1, which calls for the prompt and inexpensive disposition of litigation in the federal courts. The 2015 amendment to Rule 1 provides specifically for proportionality—that the cost of litigation (including preserving ESI and shaping discovery to focus only on the evidence needed to dispose of the legal issues) must be kept in balance with the amount in controversy. No more $40,000 discovery tab for a $50,000 case. On the other hand, judges considering motions about discovery costs have been alerted by the Committee Notes to require facts rather than fretting from the lawyers.

Your authors are hopeful that that a teamwork approach to the litigation hold, based on team members with a mutual understanding of the process from all perspectives will ease the burden of effective evidence preservation and discovery.

CHAPTER 2

Preserving, Not Corrupting—Hold It!

HOW FAR DOES PRESERVATION STRETCH? INFORMATION VERSUS EVIDENCE

In the modern Anglo-American legal system, litigation is the process of weighing the competing versions of the "facts" about a dispute. The whole point of the process is to find and evaluate the information that is both reliable and to-the-point (that is, in legalese, relevant). Lots of information surrounding a dispute may be interesting, sometimes even entertaining. A judge, however, will only be looking for the important information from a dispute resolution perspective. That important information is evidence. Evidence is any reliable information likely to assist in resolution of a dispute (Black's Law Dictionary). Only evidence goes to a jury, through the intricate series of filters that comprise a modern trial. Witnesses are examined and cross-examined. Documents are vigorously examined for completeness and reliability. The evidence the jury finally considers in reaching a verdict should be the truth, the whole truth and nothing but the truth.

That can only happen when the parties to the lawsuit hold on to the evidence they control. The litigation "hold" required by the Rules is about one thing—preserving all information that is reasonably likely to be evidence.

The Hold Notice—A Brief Introduction

The notice to hold (preserve) evidence comes in two general forms. In the "internal" form, a company sends the word throughout the organization to hold all the information related to an event. In the "external" form, lawyers for the plaintiff, or the party which will later become the plaintiff, send a written demand to the party which will become the defendant, informing the defendant-to-be that litigation is on the way about a specific event and demanding that all information related to that event must be preserved.

Our concern here is the internal hold notice, because the obligation to preserve evidence arises with the event, not with the receipt of a letter from a possible legal opponent. The external hold notice is a good idea, but it is not the action demanded by the Rules.

11

CONTENTS

The opposite of preservation is, in legal terms, spoliation. On the criminal law side, spoliation is called evidence-tampering, and it will get you an extremely unpleasant conversation with a person who carries a badge. On the civil law side, spoliation can get you an extremely unpleasant conversation with a judge, or worse. On the tech side, it is called data corruption. More on all of that momentarily. But, whichever floor of the courthouse you are headed for, the concept is the same.

One more legal term to keep in mind: negligence. This is the polite legal term for generalized stupidity. It is a special brand of carelessness, technically (in legalese), the failure to take the ordinary care that a reasonable person would take under the same or similar circumstances (Black's Law Dictionary). It won't get you off the hook for spoliation, but it may lessen your punishment. Or it may not, as we will see.

A HISTORICAL FOOTNOTE

A brief look back gives us a notion of how the legal concept of preserving evidence, and its opposite, spoliation, have developed.

According to the Oxford English Dictionary, the earliest published use of the term "spoliation" in English comes from the ecclesiastical court records of the 15th century. In that early form of the word, spoliation was the act of taking the financial and other benefits of a church position that belonged to someone else by employing a pretense of being the rightful owner of the benefice. It was essentially an act of fraud rather than destruction.

By the 16th century, "spoliation" had changed its meaning as it entered the general public vocabulary. It covered acts such as robbery, looting, plunder, and similar forms of taking another's property by violence. We find early variants such as "spoils of war" as a polite description of looting.

In the 18th century, as printed documents became widely available and general literacy grew, English legal usage settled on spoliation as an act of destroying or tampering with a physical document so as to "spoil" or destroy its value as evidence. (Please feel free to drop your bookmark here and spend a moment looking at the spoliation-related vocabulary in the Oxford English Dictionary.)

IN THE PRESENT, SPOLIATION VERSUS INTEGRITY OF EVIDENCE

In modern legal practice, each party to a dispute has a right to present its own evidence to the court and a right to see all of the other party's evidence, both the good and the bad, before trial.

In the case of evidence, each party has a duty (legal obligation) to preserve evidence. The duty is not owed to the other side, but to the court. The duty is to present all its evidence accurately, first to the other side before trial and then to the court during trial. If the court cannot rely on the accuracy and reliability of the evidence, there is no point in having courts or trials.

Note that this duty that all parties owe to the court, the duty of preserving and producing all reliable evidence, binds both the complaining and defending parties, although most of the reported spoliation cases involve defendants.

It is also worth noting that the duty to accurately preserve and deliver evidence binds the client, including management personnel and in-house counsel, as well as outside litigation counsel. A major bad act involving corrupted data will subject a wide group of individuals to punishment. "How was I supposed to know" is not going to work as an excuse for any of them. We will have more later about each attorney's independent duty to preserve evidence.

In order for evidence to be presented to the court, it first has to be identified as evidence—information directly related to the dispute—by the party that controls it. Then it has to be preserved accurately, so that what the opponent and the court see is the real information, not the information as the party (or its lawyers) would like it to be.

If information is interesting, entertaining, embarrassing, but not useful in resolving the dispute at hand, then the party in control of it is perfectly free to manipulate it, frame it, give it away, or destroy it completely by any convenient means. No one ever has a duty to preserve irrelevant information. If it is not evidence, no one cares.

Following the same logical path, no one has a duty to preserve evidence of a dispute that cannot exist. As a completely random example, your company cannot (successfully) be sued by a customer who dislikes the color scheme of your service vehicles. Your company can certainly be sued over the vehicle color scheme by a competitor already in the same market with the same distinctive color scheme on its vehicles. This is why early and accurate analysis of the exact scope of a potential dispute is critical.

This is also why the concept of the triggering event is critical, and why we will discuss it in detail. This is the moment to concentrate on evidence documenting the event.

As technology has developed through the twentieth and twenty-first centuries, paper as an essential element of a "document" has given way to the concept of electronically stored information—ESI.

As soon as there were more than two electronic documents in the known universe, ESI storage systems became convenient, then necessary, then critical. In addition more volume equals more complexity, leading us to the era of Big Data and the Internet of Things. More of that later, also.

For the most part, the same duty to preserve information applies to both paper documents and ESI. Spoliation can only occur when a (potential) party to litigation has a duty to preserve the information as evidence. We will discuss that link to triggering events later.

Shortly, we will discuss a few of our favorite cases demonstrating spoliation of ESI, and explore the range of bad things that can happen to people who indulge in corrupting ESI when they have a duty to preserve it.

Evidence must be in the party's control, although it may be in someone else's possession. For our purposes, this means that the party either has direct access to the ESI, or has the right to demand access from whoever has actual control. This includes the Cloud and similar off-site storage of ESI, which we will be talking about later, as well as special problems with outsourced IT and/or data operations. The point is that the evidence must be somewhere that the party can obtain access.

Intent—a person's mental state—is a crucial element of spoliation. A party will generally not be punished for loss of ESI through simple negligence (carelessness). Spoliation requires a higher level of bad intent than mere stupidity or general carelessness. The party crying foul needs to show the court that the loss was because of bad faith, gross negligence, or intentional failure of preservation.

The complaining party must also show that it has actually been prejudiced (harmed) in putting on its case by the disappearance of the evidence. If there are five items of evidence showing essentially the same thing, the loss of one, or even four, may save the bad actor from punishment because there was no real damage to the other party, even by obvious and egregious destruction of evidence. However, as we will show later, no one should count on "no harm, no foul" as a defense to punishment for spoliation.

Effective (sanction-proof) ESI preservation requires two things: a clear plan to issue a hold notice throughout the organization and to comply with it, plus proof that the plan was followed all up and down the line within the organization. The focus of this book is that hold notice and that plan, and how to make them work for you in the trial preparation process.

Also, just for the record, a "sanction" is legalese for a punishment ordered by the court, for bad acts during trial preparation or during the trial itself. A sanction order is completely separate from determining the merits, the actual facts, and outcome of the underlying dispute. It is possible for you to engage in seriously bad behavior with the evidence and still win. But do not bet on it. The law is not on your side when you start down that road. Judges do keep score, and they do have ways to rip your winning case out from under you, as we are about to show you.

BAD ACTS: EXAMPLES FROM REPORTED CASES

Bad acts can have bad consequences, from the inconvenient to the catastrophic.

In lawsuits, the bad consequences depend on the trial judge's sense of proportion. Inconveniencing the other side is not in the same league with deliberate destruction of evidence combined with perjury about that destruction. And skating close to the edge in following the Rules is not in the same league with deliberately ignoring several successive orders from the court to produce specific electronic evidence.

As you know, discovery is the process of gathering evidence from the other side before trial, including by oral depositions (live questioning of witnesses before trial), requests to see specific groups of documents and/or physical objects, interrogatories (written questions to be answered under oath), and other methods set out in the Rules. This is the point in the process where spoliation is discovered.

Spoliation includes more than just destruction. It includes mutilation, or alteration of evidence, as well as concealment and misdirection, failure to produce an item of evidence when required to do so, failure to produce the complete contents of an item, and failure to preserve evidence for later production.

Spoliation comes in two general categories: by omission of evidence—allowing the evidence to disappear or concealing it, and by commission—actively altering or destroying evidence due to, among other things, improper handling. Both of these methods of spoliation can range from careless and ignorant loss to deliberate and widespread destruction. Thus, the range of punishments will reflect not only the range of loss but also the spoliator's intent.

Destruction by Omission

Here are a few examples of destruction by omission, taken from court records summarized in one of our favorite sources, *Moore's Federal Practice* (Matthew Bender, third ed.), an up-to-date summary of hundreds of federal cases, organized by each part of each of the Rules.

Each of these failures is from a different case, and each resulted in at least one sanctions order by the trial court.

When discovery goes bad, the judge will generally require the offender to document in detail its exact efforts to preserve and produce evidence. As you can see later, courtesy of *Moore's*, that is where the fun begins (from a forensic expert's perspective, that is). In each of these cases, sanctions ensued.

- Defendant megacorp failed to provide any affidavits of its efforts to locate relevant ESI, after it was ordered to conduct and document a thorough search to produce relevant ESI at its own expense.

- Defendant failed to show that it had searched the electronic records stored at different subsidiaries involved in the actions in dispute.
- Plaintiff failed to submit any affidavit from a knowledgeable individual verifying the scope of its ESI search, its efforts to locate documents, explaining its inability to identify and produce documents, and the dates on which documents were deleted or removed from computers. In addition, the plaintiff failed to respond to discovery requests.
- Defendant (1) did not suspend automatic biweekly email destruction, (2) insufficiently distributed the hold notice (to a limited group of top managers only) and failed to follow up on compliance supervision for seven months after the triggering event, and (3) during litigation the corporation failed to monitor preservation efforts by its employees for continued compliance with the hold notice.
- A party failed to stop an automatic document-destruction feature from operating on the party's computer system during litigation.
- A litigation hold covering only four key players (individuals having potentially discoverable information) was deliberately inadequate, since the opposing party had identified 100 other individuals as key players during initial Rule 26(a) disclosures.
- Defendant failed to suspend routine deletion of ESI in the computer of a former employee upon the employee's separation from the company, when the former employee had been specifically identified as a key player.
- Defendant failed to maintain computer hard drives of former employees when management knew they had played significant roles in the activities that were the subject of litigation.

Spoliation by omission also includes failure to produce ESI, failure to collect and provide details to support summarized information, ignoring company systems outside of a company's main business office, allowing the deletion of data by improperly allowing access to computers by individuals who should not have access, and by failure to understand the ESI systems, so as to block effective searches for ESI evidence.

Destruction by Commission

Spoliation also occurs by commission, actively altering or deleting ESI. This routinely happens by improperly handling ESI and the systems in which it is created and stored. For example, from *Moore's*:

- Defendant's employees were allowed to continue using a laptop for several months after litigation was filed, although the management knew or should have known that that the laptop contained relevant ESI that would be destroyed or deleted by such continued use.
- A party deliberately converted or transferred data to an inaccessible format.

- Data on the individual defendant's computer was altered or destroyed when the corporate defendant continued to use it, deleting files—sending them to unallocated space on the hard drive so that the computer could overwrite the files with new data.
- Defendant selectively preserved some ESI and destroyed other ESI.
- Individual defendant (owner of the corporate defendant) obtained access to the company's computers and deleted thousands of emails, as well as other ESI, including product drawings and other documents stolen from a competitor (the plaintiff), and ordered outside contractors to do the same. He did not give any hold notice or preservation instruction at all to corporate employees, despite several obvious triggering events both pre-litigation and during litigation. When challenged about ESI destruction, he said he deleted the ESI to "store them in the delete file". The corporate defendant's in-house IT "expert" of several years (the spouse of another management-level employee) was not told to "hold" ESI, even after issuance of a specific hold order by the judge. An outside litigation consultant was not told that there was any hold plan, so merely "sampled" ESI in the company's current (new) system for relevant ESI, without examining or incorporating the ESI in the legacy (former) system. The in-house IT person (who was without any certifications or advanced training) allowed massive deletions and used a "defragging" cleanup program on the main system as well as on the backup system, overwriting all deleted ESI.

As you have noticed, failure to control an automated file-purging system promptly and adequately is a common thread in many spoliation cases. Since all of these cases resulted in sanctions, failure to manage your technology is clearly not a useful excuse.

Destruction of ESI results from bad management decisions (sometimes by lack of any decision), lack of adequate supervision of employees, and even from selection of inadequately trained forensic or e-discovery "experts", whether they are in-house IT personnel, contractors, or consultants.

Experts (Or Not)
Even this very limited selection of cases from *Moore's* shows that having no IT expert at all is a bad choice. But what about the alternatives?

In-house IT Employees
Judges have made it plain that employees designated as IT personnel probably will not be "experts" when the question of adequate preservation arises. In discovery conflicts, the parties must present proof that they complied with their preservation duty and their own hold notices. Such compliance is difficult to prove without actual experts.

This is particularly difficult if the in-house IT employees are not properly notified of the scope of the preservation plan and the specific terms of any associated court orders.

In addition, in-house employees without expert or system-proficiency certificates, advanced IT training, etc, may be considered unreliable as "experts" to testify on questions of appropriate preservation techniques, especially if the employees have inadequately managed system issues in the past, or are not solely in control of the ESI systems.

Outside IT "Consultants"

Judges are likely to find that self-styled "consultants" who are inadequately credentialed in both systems management and ESI segregation and preservation are also inadequate to prove that the preservation compliance was adequately directed.

Even well-credentialed IT consultants will not be able to prove compliance, if they are unfamiliar with any associated legacy systems, or are not solely in control of the ESI systems.

Worse yet is the choice to rely on a regular outside IT vendor, especially one who failed to retrieve complete data on prior occasions.

Reliance on an unsupported "expert" statement that ESI cannot be retrieved simply raises further issues of the competence of the "expert" rather than resolving the underlying preservation question. The judge is looking for reasonableness in selecting preservation experts, not convenience or cost.

Outside IT Litigation Consultants

Litigation consultants who hold themselves out as experts in IT may not shield a party from spoliation sanctions if the consultant fails to inquire clearly about the scope of the hold plan and the scope of the consultant's job. An improperly-instructed outside consultant may fail to adequately hold all ESI by merely "sampling" data. The consultant also may fail to preserve ESI properly, if the consultant is not fully informed about legacy systems and storage devices not directly connected to the main computer system, such as external hard drives, jump drives and similar transfer devices, laptops, process systems at other locations, as well as information in the possession of corporate subsidiaries or other corporate divisions, contractors, etc.

THE OTHER ROUTE—DESTRUCTION WITH PERMISSION

Many of the disasters we described earlier could have been avoided if the offending party had chosen to immediately consult with a properly credentialed forensic IT expert, and to go straight to the judge to get the cost of preservation shifted to the party requesting the evidence. Here are two mega-dollar examples from *Moore's*, but the consideration is proportionately the same for mid-sized and small businesses.

- To mitigate the high cost of extreme-volume ESI storage, which would have required an entire separate storage system, megacorp defendant was permitted by the court to continue deleting ESI in the ordinary course of business, provided that the hard (paper) copies of relevant ESI were made and kept (thus avoiding metadata issues, about which we will have more to say later).
- Suspension of all email purging for the entire megacorp defendant, as requested by the plaintiff, was found by the court to be unreasonable. The parties were instructed to draft a limited preservation order specifying a procedure to identify groups of emails for further examination.

Note that in both these cases, the automated destruction of ESI was done after obtaining permission from the court, not by actions taken by the defendant on its own and announced later during a discovery conflict. Whoever said that asking for forgiveness is better than asking for permission was dead wrong.

CURATIVE ACTION AND SANCTIONS

You now have a sense of the wide variety of bad choices management can make about preserving ESI, or failing to preserve it, or deliberately destroying it. Here is a brief sample of judicial thinking about what may happen, when a litigant aggravates a federal judge by spoliation.

The General Theory—Courts Must Maintain Their Integrity

Every court—whether at the federal, state, or local level—has the obligation to control the parties who appear there, so that there is an orderly process in resolving disputes. A court does this through its inherent (automatic) authority to manage cases and control the orderly administration of justice and to preserve the integrity of the justice system as a whole. This is why the preservation duty arises before the filing of a lawsuit. No action by the court, no order to preserve evidence, is needed to trigger the duty to hold evidence or to invoke the court's right to enforce the integrity of the judicial system.

The Balancing Act

Judges have a very wide variety of choices in deciding how to punish a spoliator. But there are some guidelines, developed through many years of case law. The key, as in the rest of the judicial system, is to balance the harm and the punishment. No one is going to federal prison for allowing deletion of all the duplicate copies of an email as long as one copy remains. No one is even going to be yelled at for such destruction, because there has been no prejudice (legal damage) to the other party's ability to put on its case.

The court looks at the guilty act, but also at the level of damage to the other side. Truly, no harm no foul. But if there is harm, then it is not just the corporate bank account that is on the line in punishment. The continued existence of the lawsuit may be on the line also.

Appeals courts looking at various punishments issued by trial courts agree that the level of sanctions, whether monetary or otherwise, is a matter for the trial court to decide on a case-by-case basis, weighing the degree of destruction as well as the degree of prejudice to the other party.

In addition, the trial court must consider whether the spoliator had notice of the relevance of the destroyed ESI and whether the spoliator actually had a duty to preserve the ESI at the time of the destruction. The trial court must give weight to the party's obligation to issue an internal hold notice as soon as it receives information indicating a triggering event. The court will consider whether the notice was widely distributed within the organization and whether its implementation was adequately monitored. Ignorance of the need to disable auto-delete systems might excuse punishment of the front-line IT personnel, but it adds to the evidence that the supervisors in management (including in-house counsel) deliberately disregarded their duties to the court to preserve the destroyed ESI. Courts do not expect in-house IT personnel to be lawyers. Courts do expect lawyers to very clearly inform management and all other appropriate employees, regardless of status, that the hold procedure is mandatory, not just a quaint notion.

The trial court must also consider the cost burden of various levels of preservation, particularly by balancing preservation costs against the amount in controversy in the suit. It is obvious that this consideration should be raised at the beginning of the trial process, when the discovery order and schedule are being set. A party should not be burdened with $50,000 in ESI identification and storage costs for a $60,000 lawsuit. Those costs might be perfectly acceptable in a $5.5 million suit, however.

In determining a sanction after bad acts by a party, the court must conduct this proportionality analysis, along with considerations of the individual spoliators' state of mind, and the degree of relevance of the vanished evidence. For example, transfer of ESI to storage media that the other party could not access without enormous expense tends to tip the balance toward punishment, reflected in not shifting that expense to the requesting party.

The structure of Rules 34 and 37 is plain. These Rules also kick in before the rest of the pretrial rules. The duty to preserve ESI does not arise when the lawsuit papers arrive at the General Counsel's desk. The Rule requires action to preserve ESI from the moment a reasonable business person would expect legal trouble was coming. The trial court will consider whether the company, including both its in-house and trial counsel, complied with the Rule requirements to issue an adequate pre-litigation hold notice to the organization, and to supervise continuing compliance by all employees, both before the lawsuit began and during the pre-trial process.

The Hammer Falls

Here is, generally, the order of severity of spoliation sanctions. Each of these requires a demonstration of intent (state of mind) worse than simple carelessness.

Note that instead of or in addition to sanctions (punishments), the court can also order curative actions, such as reopening the discovery period, allowing additional depositions, and other efforts to restore the balance of the evidence after spoliation is identified.

- Ordering payment of the nonspoliator's attorneys' fees and expenses related to additional necessary discovery, as well as for the fees and expenses of the spoliation motions;
- Ordering payment of additional monetary awards in addition to attorneys' fees and expenses, especially for continuing or repeat offenses;
- Issuing preclusion orders, which prevent the spoliator from offering certain evidence of its own, especially excluding the spoliator's expert evidence regarding the destroyed ESI;
- Ordering specific critical facts to be established in favor of the nonspoliator without the need to put on evidence to prove those facts;
- Excluding certain defenses (for defendant spoliator) or claims (for plaintiff spoliator) in their entirety, preventing the spoliator from putting on any evidence for those claims or defenses;
- Giving permissible inference instructions to the jury, which permit them to assume destroyed ESI was evidence favorable to the nonspoliator;
- Giving adverse inference instruction to the jury, directing them to assume destroyed ESI was evidence favorable to the nonspoliator, and allowing them to assume whatever else they wish about the spoliator from that;
- Dismissing plaintiff-spoliator's case entirely, or awarding default judgment against defendant-spoliator—a win without a trial for the nonspoliator and the death penalty without a trial for the spoliator.

For example (from *Moore's*, of course), a megacorp defendant refused to follow several orders from the court to produce ESI. Then it refused to follow an order to identify all the computers used in the business, so that a forensic expert could be sent in to inspect them. Further refusals and delay followed. Result:

the court entered a default judgment against the defendant without a trial, awarding the plaintiff $5.4 million. The award of that judgment without trial, and the amount, were upheld on appeal.

Another court pointed out that default judgment against the defendant without trial was proper, because there was clear and convincing evidence of deliberate destruction of critical ESI evidence.

The Cell Door Slams, Occasionally

In general, civil trial courts hearing disputes between two parties (as opposed to criminal cases) cannot sentence people to jail terms.

But people have been inspired to aggravate judges enough to find ways around that restriction. For example, an individual defendant was sentenced to two years in prison for his continuing refusal to obey a series of court orders to pay the opposing party's fees and expenses for document destruction, while he continued to destroy ESI of the corporate defendant he controlled. The prison sentence was not a criminal sentence, according to the sentencing judge. It was for civil contempt of the court. The offender could be released at any time by paying the accumulated fees and expenses.

EACH ATTORNEY'S INDEPENDENT PRESERVATION DUTY

Most of the profoundly bad decisions we have discussed in this chapter were decisions made by management personnel, sometimes with the agreement of in-house counsel. We have to ask, where were these spoliators' trial lawyers— the people who have to stand in front of the judge when the destruction comes to light—when all this was going on?

When a lawsuit becomes reasonably foreseeable (a triggering event), as well as during the pre-trial discovery process, every individual attorney associated with a party has an independent duty to the court to see to preservation of ESI. Pre-litigation, obviously, trial counsel is likely not involved. Therefore, the burden falls on both in-house corporate counsel (who know about the obligation) to clearly and firmly advise senior management (who know about the looming conflict). Fulfilling this duty to preserve evidence includes much more than sending a memo to other members of management that "a hold on evidence should now be put in place." (An appeals court judge took the time to point out specifically that the language just quoted was far less than adequate.)

The lawyer's duty is to properly define the exact scope of the likely lawsuit, to identify the information needed in the litigation hold, and to implement the hold by an adequately detailed notice, including active monitoring for continuing compliance. The duty to make preservation happen, and see that it continues to happen, is owed by every in-house lawyer associated with the pre-litigation situation analysis from the moment of the triggering event. The preservation duty applies as well to each individual litigation attorney as soon as they are employed. Neither group can safely assume the other will handle the hold process. No individual lawyer gets to assume that duty is someone else's problem.

Many judges have pointed out the same obvious points to attorneys regarding their individual and independent duty of preservation. Considering the number of times the same points are repeated in case summaries, they bear repeating here. Consider yourself on notice, lawyers. Your duty to preserve evidence beats your duty to make management happy.

THE KEY TO THE HOLD NOTICE: NAME THE KEY PLAYERS ASAP

Each attorney with a client (including in-house counsel) is obligated to actively oversee issuance of a detailed, understandable notice, to be circulated to all employees who might possibly have any connection to any "key player" (any individual connected with the dispute).

The notice must identify each key player, and describe the exact kinds of ESI related to the key players that need to be preserved. Here is the key to the effective notice: it has to be effective. That means it has to identify people and ESI in a way that normal human beings, especially including the IT staff, can understand so those normal human beings can make it happen.

Each attorney involved with the preparation and distribution of the hold notice must also supervise implementation of the hold and then monitor it for continued compliance. This is an effort requiring long-term coordination, so that adequate (read, understandable) notice of the immediate and ongoing hold activity gets to every employee who might reasonably be involved in maintaining ESI evidence related to the triggering event.

This includes a related duty to see that all outside vendors associated with the company's ESI are alerted at the same time.

More Thoughts About "Keys" to an Effective Hold—The Wider View

Management (including in-house counsel) must communicate the litigation hold to employees associated with *all* potential key players—to all the individuals likely to have control of information related to the individuals and events associated with likely upcoming litigation and litigation already in progress.

The notice group includes all employees associated with potential key players, such as secretaries, assistants (and former secretaries and assistants), even file clerks, if those individuals had hands-on contact with any key player's ESI. Think how often a middle manager says to his assistant or secretary, "Send a memo to Joe telling him this information about my conversation today with Fred." The ESI will have been generated from the assistant's or secretary's workstation, not the manager's. The assistant and the secretary need to be on the list of individuals whose ESI needs to be preserved long enough to sort through it. And the assistant may also have a secretary. Is the assistant or the secretary a key player in the underlying dispute, in the sense of being a likely witness in court? Probably not. Is the assistant or secretary a person with control of ESI evidence? Probably yes.

If you have gotten this far, you already know this: management's (including in-house counsel's) failure to issue written instructions communicated to all appropriate employees (not just a select few department heads) advising them of the issues in litigation and their individual duties to preserve ESI is sanctionable (punishable by the judge). It is "inexcusable" (quoting a judge, of course) for management (including in-house counsel) to fail to warn employees to preserve documents known to be relevant to litigation.

Among their duties, the attorneys in in-house counsel's office must actively assist management to promptly and clearly identify all "key players." These are the individuals (regardless of status) who may have written, received, or controlled any ESI related to the subjects of the litigation, including subjects of likely future litigation.

Clearly, in this context "key" does not refer to an individual's status in the organization or at the center of the dispute. It means they are individuals who have generated or managed ESI that may be related to the dispute in any way. They are key evidence controllers. The attorneys must supervise expansion of this key-players list as necessary to reflect disclosure of persons who are likely to have discoverable information (under Rule 26, which we discussed earlier), and refine it to meet a reasonable reading of likely discovery requests.

The lawyer's duty includes supervising and monitoring a comprehensive search for ESI, even ESI that is normally inaccessible (such as in legacy systems and back-up storage).

Each attorney is responsible to see that the "client" (a term we will explore in depth shortly) is fully advised of the client's duty to the court to preserve ESI, both before and during litigation, through the hold procedure.

Each attorney is also obligated to take all reasonable steps to monitor compliance with the hold procedure, so the client and attorney can jointly produce all responsive ESI evidence, including ESI produced or received by employees who are no longer at the company.

As we have pointed out, the hold notice drafted by counsel and sent down the chain of command from management must be clear enough for all normally intelligent human beings to understand, so that the actual working individuals who receive the notice can take effective actions to preserve ESI. A paragraph of lawyer-speak will not suffice.

Attorneys who fail to completely communicate the exact nature and process for preservation are subject to monetary as well as nonmonetary public sanctions by the court. Here are a few more examples from *Moore's*.

An attorney who knew his client had no documents retention policy at the time of a triggering event was sanctioned. His violation? He failed to "cause a retention policy to be adopted" which would have prevented ESI from being destroyed.

An outside litigation attorney was sanctioned for his failure to fully and clearly advise in-house corporate counsel of the full scope of the litigation hold procedure—the court stated that the lawyer should have known that a short memo to management to "save evidence" was obviously inadequate.

In a truly egregious case, the attorneys for a party were reprimanded on the record, and their client was ordered to pay $8.5 million (yes, million) to the opposing party as a pre-trial punishment, after the court received proof that the attorneys had assisted their client in "intentionally hiding or recklessly ignoring relevant documents, ignoring or rejecting numerous warning signs that (the client's) document search was inadequate, and blindly accepting (the client's) unsupported assertions that its documents search was adequate."

And here is a direct experience from one of your authors: A federal trial court reported a lawyer to his state's licensing authority for discipline after he failed to examine critical financial ESI to confirm that the "evidence" he submitted to the court at a hearing was in fact identical to the financial documents his client provided earlier to the client's lender, the opposing party. The tax return documents the client gave to the lender were already in the lawyer's possession before the hearing, marked as the lender's exhibits. The lawyer offered a set of tax documents that were clearly nonidentical. Your author, at the court's order, inquired to the IRS about which set of documents was the "as filed" return. The IRS report: no return at all was filed for that year. The judge was supremely displeased. The attorney was also permanently suspended from practice in the federal courts of his district.

At this point, feel free to consult *Moore's* for more Rule 37 and Rule 37(e) details, and to check the names of the parties. You do not need to be a lawyer to appreciate some of the corporate names you will see.

ZUBULAKE, PENSION COMMITTEE, RIMKUS AND MORE

We are going to explore in depth several cases that have come to stand for the major issues in ESI preservation. These cases have interpreted the duty to preserve and produce ESI in lawsuits. And they have wrestled with what the appropriate curative actions and/or punishment should be. (BTW, the wrestling continues, including a notable public tussle in 2014 over amendment of Federal Rule 37(e). We will get to the outcome momentarily.)

Lawyers reading this should already know the evidentiary take-away of these cases, so we are not going to wade too deeply into the legal details, or do legalese things like pinpoint cites. We are looking for the information everyone should know, from trial counsel to the IT personnel, who are told to "just do whatever" to prevent routine destruction of ESI, store potentially huge amounts of data, and still keep the company's computer systems operating. (Another legalese note: we prefer to cite to Federal Rules Decisions, a specialized series of court case reports that deal specifically with the Federal Rules. Lawyers know how to use these citations to find the same cases in other places. Where no F.R.D. cite is readily available, we do what we can to get you to the right place, which will usually be LEXIS or F. Supp). Nonlawyers who would like to join in the fun by at least reading the fact statements in these opinions, please feel free to have your lawyer colleagues get on this for you. It will be worth it, we promise.

Zubulake (I–V)

Early in 2003, Laura Zubulake, a former financial trader at UBS Warburg in New York City, filed a federal lawsuit in the Southern District of New York against her ex-employer for gender discrimination. We note that this lawsuit was filed before Federal Rule 37 was amended in 2006 to add a specific provision about electronic evidence—that no one would be punished for loss of ESI through "routine, good-faith operation" of a computer system. At the time of the Zubulake lawsuit, the general rules about production of paper documents were being stretched to cover ESI. At that point, "all" documents just meant "all" documents, regardless of the form in which they were created or maintained.

During pretrial evidence discovery, federal trial judge Shira Scheindlin issued an amazing FIVE separate detailed opinions between May 2003 and July 2004. Four of them zeroed in on UBS's failures to produce the ESI that was requested by Zubulake's lawyers.

In the early opinions, Judge Scheindlin responded to UBS's demands that Zubulake should have to pay for retrieving emails related to the case from the UBS electronic archives, because the emails had become inaccessible to the regular computer system. Retrieving them would be, the UBS lawyers said, enormously expensive. The judge ordered UBS to produce all responsive emails from various servers and back-up tapes at its own expense. The cost-shifting determination was to follow when the actual scope and cost of the production was known. (*Zubulake I*: 217 F.R.D. 309 (S.D.N.Y. 2003) [May 13, 2003]; *Zubulake II*: [not an ESI opinion]; *Zubulake III*: 216 F.R.D. 280 (S.D.N.Y. 2003) [Jul. 24, 2003].)

By *Zubulake IV* (220 F.R.D. 212 (S.D.N.Y. 2003) [Oct. 22, 2003]), the UBS lawyers announced that not only were the back-up tapes missing, the Zubulake-related emails were deleted from other storage. We deduce from the tone of the order that the judge's eyeballs were bulging out in exasperation. She determined that UBS knew it had a duty to preserve the emails and other ESI, and that it knew about that duty well before Zubulake filed her lawsuit. But UBS failed to comply with that duty.

Worse yet, the Judge pointed out that UBS violated its own documents retention policy in disposing of Zubulake-related ESI. Without that violation the ESI would still have been in existence. Her unavoidable conclusion: UBS deliberately destroyed evidence.

However, the Judge pointed out, there was another problem. Zubulake was required to show by other evidence that the destroyed evidence supported her claims—a requirement for severe punishments. Without access to the ESI, she could not put on any such proof. The solution? UBS had to pay the cost for her lawyers to reexamine certain witnesses about the destruction and about certain newly produced ESI.

The Judge specifically ruled out the punishment of instructing the jury at trial to assume whatever was destroyed was bad for the spoliator, UBS, because Zubulake could not prove the lost ESI was directly related to the dispute as well as favorable to her.

In the tone of the *Zubulake* V opinion, nine months later (229 F.R.D. 422 (S.D.N.Y. 2004); 2004 WL 1620866 (S.D.N.Y. Jul. 20, 2004)), we can hear the whistle of the gavel flying through the air toward UBS's lawyers as well as their client. Zubulake's lawyers had pointed out that UBS produced the withheld ESI long after the original pretrial evidence discovery deadline, prejudicing the Zubulake lawyers' ability to prepare for the scheduled trial date. In addition, UBS never produced some emails whose existence was already known, including emails directly related to conversations about Zubulake.

After hearing UBS's side of this latest dispute, Judge Scheindlin concluded that UBS deliberately destroyed emails directly related to the dispute, and did so after she ordered them to be produced. She informed the parties that in light of the post-order destruction, the jury would be instructed to presume the destroyed documents supported Zubulake's claims rather than UBS's defense. She also ordered UBS, the client, to pay the fees and costs for Zubulake's attorneys to bring the destruction to the court's attention.

The Judge then turned to the UBS lawyers. She determined that the lawyers shared the blame with their client for the document destruction. The lawyers, she noted, knew they had an independent duty to identify evidence (regardless of its form) and see to its preservation, as well as the duty to produce it during pretrial discovery. She stated, "Counsel must take affirmative steps to monitor compliance so that all the sources of discoverable information are identified and searched." She also, notably, pointed out that litigators must guarantee preservation of ESI as well as paper evidence, by initiating a "litigation hold" and by seeing that the preservation requirement was effectively communicated to all individuals within the client organization. Not "should consider" doing that. Must do that.

The 2006 Rules Amendments on ESI

Time went by. Judges, lawyers, and businesses all struggled with the technical as well as financial burdens of preserving what they hoped would be the right ESI after triggering events. Or they just ignored triggering events and hoped that an aggressive claim or defense would carry the day. It was messy. It was confusing. It was guaranteed to aggravate judges everywhere.

The Federal Rules were amended in 2006 by the Judicial Conference of the United States, the organization to which all federal judges belong, through its Committee on Rules of Practice and Procedure. The amendments were adopted in Apr.12, 2006, effective Dec. 1, 2006. Originally Rule 37 subsection (f), now subsection (e), was an attempt to limit some of the ESI confusion.

The new ESI provision said, under the caption Failure to Provide Electronically Stored Information: "Absent exceptional circumstances, a court may not impose sanctions under these rules on a party for failing to provide electronically stored information lost as a result of the routine, good-faith operation of an electronic information system."

The judges thought it was pretty clear. The Committee Notes accompanying the new provision went on at considerable length to discuss the judges' understanding of the concept of "good-faith operation". The Committee Notes made the point that "good-faith operation" includes intervening in regular system operations to prevent automatic destruction of ESI which the operator should reasonably expect to be evidence in potential or pending litigation. A "pure heart, empty head" excuse (pardon the legalese) was not going to work any longer.

The Committee Notes to the Rule 37 amendment also pointed out a crucial distinction between sanctions (which are punishments for improper behavior) and "adjustments" to the pretrial discovery process, to give the nonoffending party some other means to obtain information contained in inaccessible or destroyed ESI. Only sanctions, not adjustments, are limited by the 2006 amendment.

Regrettably, many judges failed to make that distinction in their opinions and orders. As a result, many court-ordered work-arounds in extending discovery have been referred to as sanctions against the spoliator. That trend has not been useful in helping people to understand the obligation to "hold" ESI when a lawsuit becomes likely.

ESI problems in litigation staggered on. It became clearer than ever that lawyers, both in-house counsel and trial counsel, were not making themselves clear to their clients. Management and IT personnel did not know in a practical way what the hold obligation meant to the organization (assuming the lawyers themselves understood the client's obligation or their own).

Pension Committee

In 2010, Judge Scheindlin of New York was back in the legal news with an extended opinion (88 pages of facts, followed by her conclusions) in the case of *Pension Committee of the University of Montreal Pension Plan et al. v. Banc of America Securities* (685 F. Supp. 2d 456 (S.D.N.Y. 2010); 2010 U.S. Dist. LEXIS 4546 (S.D.N.Y. Jan. 15, 2010)).

This time the defendants were blameless. The case involved 96 plaintiffs, allied in several groups. Thirteen of the plaintiffs, in various groups, could hardly have done a worse job of preserving ESI. Group by group, the Judge detailed those plaintiffs' failures to preserve their own electronic evidence *after they knew they were going to sue*. She pointed out that they were destroying, by neglect, their own ability to put on their own case.

She also pointed out, one by one, the false and/or misleading statements in the sworn declarations submitted by each plaintiff group about the nature and extent of their efforts to identify, preserve and produce ESI. The breathtaking scope of both destruction and lying was nearly beyond Judge Scheindlin's judicially-available vocabulary.

The defendant group that filed the motion for sanctions demanded that the entire lawsuit be dismissed without further ado.

The judge, taking a deep breath, agreed that while serious sanctions should be levied against the offending plaintiffs, dismissal of the entire lawsuit would be somewhat over the edge. Instead she ordered that the defendants were free to put on evidence of the breadth of the evidence destruction. She also ordered that the jury would be told that each of the plaintiffs had a duty to find and preserve the missing ESI, a duty some of them violated at a level of gross (extreme) negligence. The jurors would be free to presume, if they wished, that some or all of the lost ESI was both directly related to the dispute and favorable to the defendants.

Judge Scheindlin was seriously displeased with the offending plaintiff clients. She was also particularly outraged at the crowd of lawyers representing those plaintiffs. She zeroed in on the lawyers' collective failure to provide written litigation hold notices and see that the notices were sent through their respective client organizations, until nearly *three years after* the lawsuit was filed. That filing was itself several years after the financial activity that was in dispute. As a result the IT personnel who eventually needed to do the ESI searches within the various plaintiff organizations had no idea how to search, what to search for, where to search, and what to do with the few scraps of electronic information they did find.

Compounding the problem, some of the retrieved information did not even reach the trial attorneys until the hearing on the spoliation motion was in progress, as individuals from the various plaintiff groups testified about what they did not do with the ESI, as opposed to what their sworn declarations (presumably drafted by the lawyers) said they did.

Gross negligence by an attorney can, in some jurisdictions, cost the lawyer the right to practice in the federal courts or even his or her law license. Judge Scheindlin ruled that the lawyers' failure to send written litigation hold notices at the time of the triggering events (or any time thereafter) was, in and of itself, gross negligence. That extreme failure by the lawyers contributed significantly to the rampant disregard for evidence displayed by their clients.

Each of the lawyers individually either knew or should have known that they each had an independent duty to issue written hold notices to their clients, she determined. They knew that they were required to notify their clients in detail of the hold obligation and to identify the key players in each organization to whom the notice applied. Each lawyer should have known his or her own duty started as soon as the client started talking about the activity that led to the lawsuit and at every moment thereafter. The duty was to make the existence and scope of the ESI hold understandable to the individuals who had to carry out the actual preservation. The duty was violated not only by the clients but more importantly by the lawyers, who knew the exact scope of the hold obligation and the necessity for it, and the necessity to communicate it to the people who were paying them.

It was, she ruled, the lawyers' immediate duty to identify all the key players (whether present or former employees) within their respective corporate clients, to make absolutely sure that the deletion of all ESI ceased immediately, to obtain confirmation that backup tapes and other generally-inaccessible sources were preserved until they could be properly searched, and to regularly revisit enforcement of the hold notice with their clients, thus ensuring that the hold was being maintained.

This duty, the judge pointed out, included directing the search for actual evidence among all the pieces of electronic information, by developing appropriate key terms for electronic searches. This means that the lawyers were required by law to both understand and speak fluent "techie", a requirement that was seriously unlikely to be met by those *Pension Committee* plaintiffs' lawyers. Unlikely as that compliance was, each lawyer who failed to initiate effective and comprehensive holds, and to supervise the searches to identify preservable ESI, would be personally responsible for the failed preservation.

You would think that the lawyers, seeing the handwriting on the wall in their own blood after *Zubulake*, should have easily deduced the right thing to do, if something even sounds like it might tend toward litigation. Hire a computer forensics expert to supervise the development of the mysterious search terms and then be sure that the expert can coordinate with in-house IT personnel to get it done. You would think.

Over at the other counsel table, you would think the defendants' lawyers would be positively wiggling in their chairs with glee. You would think. You would be wrong. The defendants' lawyers now had to dance around the same legal catch-22 as the *Zubulake* plaintiff's lawyers. They had to prove that their clients were prejudiced by the loss of that specific ESI. They had to prove that the missing ESI was in the control of the spoliators, who had a duty to preserve it. They had to prove that the spoliators knew about their duty and then acted in a way that was contrary to that duty, that is, with a "culpable [legalese for guilty] state of mind." Then they had to prove that the information in the missing ESI was directly related to the underlying dispute.

Remember, "prove" means put on evidence, not just make speeches and argue about it. Obviously, the first two items, control and guilty mind, would not be terribly challenging in this case, considering the situation. Testimony showing any state of mind by management decision-makers that was worse than simple carelessness would do. The last element looked like a brick wall, however. How do you prove the relevance of something you have not seen? How can you prove the contents of a particular memo, or letter, or email, if you do not know for certain, what memos, letters, and emails even existed? The defendants had to put on evidence proving prejudice, that what was destroyed was directly related to the dispute, as well as helpful to their side. That is the tough nut where there has been destruction before anyone has reviewed the information.

The law established by previous cases in the region provided the answer for Judge Scheindlin. Case law says that when the spoliator's actions were more than simply negligent or careless, both relevance and prejudice to the injured party may be (but are not required to be) presumed. The specific circumstances of the destruction should dictate whether relevance and prejudice should or must be presumed. The spoliator is given the opportunity to show that there could not have actually been either prejudice or relevance in the missing ESI. The injured party gets to respond with its counter-evidence. Obviously, the determination must be on a case-by-case basis.

Judge Scheindlin listed off the available range of sanctions (which included both curative measures and punishments), with a reminder that the court is obliged to impose the least harsh sanction that provides a remedy. The measures go from further limited discovery, cost-shifting, so the offender pays for the additional depositions, etc (including the cost to the nonspoliator to bring the sanctions motion), fines payable to the court to offset the lost court resources caused by having to sort out the evidence destruction, special jury instructions, preclusion (preventing the spoliator from putting on certain evidence), ordering that certain facts will be taken as true without proof, and at the very far end of the range, dismissing a plaintiff spoliator's claim or entering default judgment against a defendant spoliator without further effort by the plaintiff.

The level of sanction is a balance of the spoliator's intent or state of mind and the extent of the destruction. Judge Scheindlin noted that she and her clerk spent nearly 300 hours working on this discovery dispute alone.

In this case, the Judge pointed out, each plaintiff knew far in advance that there would be a lawsuit. Yet these particular plaintiff groups chose not to save ESI that was clearly important to determining who was right and who was wrong. And their separate lawyers as well as their common trial counsel failed to take any steps at all to ensure that ESI was saved. The judge reviewed the facts about the plaintiffs' failure to preserve their own evidence, as well as the attorneys' failure to tell the clients plainly and specifically to save ESI as evidence.

She called the entire failure "gross negligence"—carelessness that just misses being reckless (deliberately ignoring a known danger). She laid the blame at the lawyers' door. The evidence destruction by each of the offending plaintiffs was not intentional, but the loss put the defendants in an impossible position. They would have to put on proof that the destroyed ESI was both directly related to the dispute and significant for their side—a double burden they could not possibly meet.

Her solution was to choose a remedy that shifted the burden to the spoliators and their attorneys. By declaring the lawyers to be grossly negligent in failing to prepare and send to their clients timely written litigation hold notices with clear instructions about their use, she found a basis for a remedy that was not merely punishment. She also announced that after all the parties put on their evidence she would instruct the jury that evidence had been destroyed by those specific plaintiffs, and the jury could presume the destroyed evidence was unfavorable to those plaintiffs. That meant that the spoliators needed to put on evidence during the trial to show that what they destroyed (even though ignorantly) was of no consequence to either side.

Meanwhile, in Texas: *Rimkus*

Judge Lee Rosenthal of the Southern District of Texas was the chair of the Committee on Rules of Practice and Procedure of the federal judiciary's Federal

Rules Advisory Committee when the 2006 amendments highlighted the issue of ESI. She was the chair again when the 2015 Rules amendments were developed between 2010 and 2014, attempting to clarify the preservation requirements. She knew intimately why further amendment was needed, soon.

In the 2010 case of *Rimkus Consulting Group, Inc. v. Cammarata* (688 F. Supp. 2d 598 (S.D. Tex. 2010); 2010 U.S. Dist LEXIS 14573 (S.D. Tex. Feb. 19, 2010)), Judge Rosenthal found clear evidence of deliberate destruction of ESI, plus inaccurate and misleading testimony about the missing evidence. Judge Rosenthal determined that instead of a determination of gross negligence and an instruction to the jury to presume both relevance and prejudice, a milder approach would suffice. Her approach: the jury should hear evidence of the destructive conduct, including the spoliator's evidence in response. Then the jury should be given the option to find, if they wished, that the destruction was intentional and done in bad faith, and that the lost evidence would have been unfavorable to the spoliators. The hammer still fell, but it was a slightly smaller hammer.

Chin v. Port Authority—A Clarification

In 2012, two years after Judge Scheindlin declared in *Pension Committee* that a lawyer's failure to send a written litigation hold notice to the client was automatically gross negligence by the lawyer, her bosses, the US Second Circuit Court of Appeals, declared in the case of *Chin v. Port Authority of New York & New Jersey* (685 F.3d 135 (2d Cir. 2012)) that a written litigation hold notice would generally be reasonable, but there could be circumstances in which it was not absolutely necessary. Therefore, failure to send a hold notice in writing, by itself, would not automatically be the basis for declaring the attorney to be grossly negligent and invoking the jury instruction used by Judge Scheindlin. (The Court of Appeals did not have a problem with the rest of her analysis or her remedy in *Pension Committee*.)

THE RULES—CONTEMPLATING AMENDMENT, AGAIN

By 2010, lawyers as well as judges were in a nationwide state of complete confusion about the actual scope of the electronic evidence provisions in the Federal Rules. Clients were in an uproar about the perceived enormous cost and disruption of shutting down automatic computer maintenance systems to prevent loss of possible evidence in possible lawsuits. There was also widespread anxiety about the related perceived enormous cost and inconvenience of maintaining separate electronic storage for everything that might be evidence in lawsuits that might or might not happen. To say nothing of the cost of lawyer and management time to develop, circulate, and police the litigation hold process itself.

And of course, there was the cost of all those forensic consultants to develop the mysterious "search terms" to find out which ESI was actually important enough to keep.

The federal judges, lawyers, and legal scholars on the Rules Standing Committee got the message. A conference was held at Duke University in 2010 to identify issues related to ESI preservation. Based on recommendations from the Duke Conference, the Committee drafted an amendment to Rule 37(e), along with various unrelated amendments to other rules. (You remember Rule 37(e), the one about no sanctions for good-faith operation of electronic systems, even if evidence got destroyed.)

The original 2013 draft of the Rule 37(e) proposed amendment was intended to set a nationwide standard for ESI preservation and specify associated sanctions, to replace the ongoing chaos. The original proposal addressed preservation of all evidence, not just ESI. It included a specific standard for determining willfulness (doing something deliberately), and described in detail the various bad things that could happen to lawyers and clients who failed to preserve evidence. It also listed the specific factors a federal trial judge would have to consider in selecting an appropriate remedy or sanction.

The public comment period on the initial proposed amendment was, as the Committee's final report described it, "strikingly, perhaps uniquely, comprehensive and vigorous." The drafters even extended the comment period from six months to seven, closing comments off in early 2014, after receiving 2,345 written comments plus statements from 120 witnesses at public hearings.

AND, BACK IN THE COURTROOM—*SEKISUI AMERICAN*

In 2014, a federal magistrate judge, refereeing a spoliation dispute in *Sekisui American Corp. v. Hart* (945 F.Supp. 2d 494 (S.D.N.Y. 2013); 2013 U.S. Dist. LEXIS 115533 (S.D.N.Y. Aug. 15, 2013—one of Judge Scheindlin's cases)), determined that although the plaintiff company failed to preserve evidence when it knew it was required to do so, the defendant did not prove that the destruction actually damaged his ability to put on his case—no harm, no foul.

Judge Scheindlin, reviewing the magistrate judge's statement of facts and conclusions on the discovery dispute, tossed the magistrate's reasoning and found that the plaintiff had to have acted willfully and deliberately, and that it was wrong to put the burden on the nonspoliator to prove that his case was harmed. Prejudice (harm) should be presumed automatically when an opponent deliberately destroys evidence, she ruled.

She also took the opportunity to blast the draft amendment to Rule 37(e) for requiring the innocent party to do the impossible—prove the contents of deliberately destroyed ESI, in order to show it was substantially prejudiced in putting on its case.

THE RULES AMENDMENT PROCESS, AGAIN—LOOKING FORWARD FROM DEC., 2015

In light of the (sometimes heated) comments from all sources, the Rules Standing Committee offered a new approach. The amendment to Rule 37(e) was revised and refocused, to address preservation of ESI only. Preservation of physical documents and other physical evidence was left to other rules.

The drafters acknowledged that the initial draft of Rule 37(e) would not solve the perceived problem of costly over-preservation. In addition, they determined that the initial draft reduced the flexibility that judges needed to address many different types of preservation failures. The revised draft amendment also removed the list of required factors that trial judges had to address in determining appropriate remedies.

The revised amendment still makes clear that simple negligence will not expose the client or lawyers to sanctions (in general). Severe measures will only be imposed where true bad faith—deliberate destruction—is proven.

Notably, the Committee stated its goals in its Report transmitting the revised Rule 37(e) amendment to the entire federal judiciary for review:

> "Two goals have inspired this work. One has been to establish greater uniformity in the ways in which federal courts respond to a loss of ESI. The courts agree unanimously that a duty to preserve ESI arises when a party reasonably anticipates litigation. But they differ significantly in the approaches taken after finding a loss of ESI that should have been preserved. A new rule that illuminates the purposes and methods of responding to the loss can do much to promote uniformity and to encourage desirable judicial responses.

> The other goal has been to relieve the pressures that have led many potential litigants to engage in what they describe as massive and costly over-preservation. An accumulation of information from many sources, including detailed examples provided in the public comments and testimony, persuasively supports the proposition that great costs are often incurred to preserve information in anticipation of litigation, including litigation that never is brought. Given the many other influences that bear on the preservation of ESI, however, it is not clear that a rule revision can provide complete relief on this front.

> ...[T]he proposed Rule 37(e) does not itself create a duty to preserve. The new rule takes the duty as it is established by case law. Cases uniformly hold that a duty to preserve information arises when litigation is reasonably

anticipated. ... The Committee Note, responding to concerns expressed in the comments, also makes clear that this rule does not affect any common-law tort remedy for spoliation that may be established by state law."

(Report to the Standing Committee, May 2, 2014, pp. 306–307 of 1132.)

The Committee Report points out specifically that the revised amendment restricts the use of severe sanctions such as adverse jury instructions, instructions to presume the missing ESI was unfavorable to the party that lost it, etc. Sanctions at that level can only be used after the court receives evidence "that the party lost the information with the intent to deprive another party of its use in the litigation." (Proposed Rule 37(e)(2); Report, p. 310.) The use of the designations "willfulness" and "bad faith" are abandoned, and the emphasis in determining the party's state of mind is on reasonableness of conduct, prejudice and the new intent-to-deprive standard.

The Committee Report noted that many written comments and witnesses complained about the costliness of perceived over-preservation. However, none of the comments or witnesses provided the Committee with actual data about preservation costs, and no one would say how much money could theoretically be saved by amending Rule 37(e) in any specific way.

Following the process required by federal regulations, the Committee passed the proposed amendments to Rule 37(e) and other rules to its parent committee and thence on to the full federal judiciary for further comments. After receiving the approved Committee Report from the Judicial Conference, the Chief Justice of the United States officially transmitted the proposed amendments and Report to Congress. The amendments became effective in all federal courts on Dec. 1, 2015.

Time will tell whether the 2015 amendment to Rule 37(e) will actually save money and/or reduce uncertainty. In the meantime, implementing an effective ESI management process is critical to a successful litigation hold. Your company's name in italics in a law book like *Moore's* is never your fondest wish.

CHAPTER 3

Incident Response While Avoiding Evidence Disaster: The Team

In this chapter, we consider your company as an organization, and identify personnel who are needed to respond effectively to a digital incident. Based on the authors' experiences, we guide you in developing your incident-response group, the Team that will work for your specific organization. This Team will be ready to act in both civil and criminal incidents, as well as in regulatory compliance investigations.

In organizations that have developed such Teams, there is a mix of disciplines and skill sets that make the Team function efficiently during each phase of the incident response. In order to achieve such results, the organization needs to understand which Team member is responsible for what area, as well as the specific kinds of information and action they control. With that distributed control, you can achieve appropriate incident and evidence management with minimal disruption to day-to-day operations.

Our primary goal in this chapter is to help you identify the skills your own Team will need for different types of events, and where to look in your organization for those skills.

The other goal of this chapter is to guide you in avoiding evidence destruction (either partial or total) during the process of collecting electronically stored information after an incident.

Evidence destruction can occur because of inadvertent operations by the IT personnel, individual users, and other parties who do not understand the litigation hold process. This lack of understanding coupled with standard operating procedures can create significant problems that, if uncorrected, will incur substantial financial and legal costs when it is necessary to recover or recreate needed evidence later.

CONTENTS

THE TEAM: FUNCTIONAL AND PROCEDURAL ISSUES

Securing ESI Repositories: A Brief Consideration of the Dark (Criminal) Side

It is important for the IT operations personnel as well as in-house counsel and management to understand the implications of damaging the physical elements of ESI storage (e.g. server, computer, etc.), when the organization becomes aware of an incident or crime. If your organization has a Chief Information Security Officer (CISO), you should already have heard this information. If you don't have one, you need to see whose job description includes these tasks.

Let us briefly consider the situation when the organization is the victim of a crime, such as a hack, denial-of-service attack, involuntary funds transfer, fraud, etc. The considerations we raise in this context are the same ones you will need to address in the civil lawsuit context, although the drama and anxiety levels will be considerably different for the Team and other personnel.

When a criminal incident targeting the organization occurs, the application of best practices in IT methodology is critical. Once the offending machine(s) are identified and located by IT, by analyzing both the external and internal network traffic, the best practice is to isolate the offending portions of the system from the rest of the network.

Isolation can be accomplished using a number of different methods. One is to physically disconnect the network connection at the machine or the wall. Another method is to access the network switch providing service and set the port into loopback mode. These methods keep the machine from communicating with the attackers but maintain the operational state of the system until the volatile data can be properly collected prior to an orderly shutdown.

A major mistake made by the inexperienced incident responders is to try to triage the problem as soon as an affected machine is identified, without disconnecting it from the network.

Another major error is to introduce or install software to clean up or find the malware prior to collection of volatile data. In today's world, most malware is designed with antiforensic capabilities. That means that if it senses the responder is trying to shut it down, defeat it, clean it, etc., the malware will go into a protection state or could be designed to destroy the system by using techniques that destroy the BIOS, the disk controller, or associated functions (such as encryption). That situation will make data recovery very difficult.

Obviously it is not just important but critical to provide a minimum of training to all individuals with access to any part of the system before there is a criminal incident such as a hack. This ensures that "helpful" but poorly trained individuals do not destroy evidence (or worse, destroy the functionality of the entire system) in their haste to stop the criminal incident. Every employee should receive brief instruction in recognizing when "something is very wrong" and designating the emergency contact personnel in IT and management. This reminder needs to be refreshed periodically so that both the IT and non-IT employees remain aware of the correct response sequence. Just as with the benefit of fire drills in an actual physical emergency, computer system emergency training will pay off by avoiding a doubled-up disaster.

When to Act in Criminal Incidents: When There is Suspicion of Misconduct

This book does not pretend to teach the techniques of monitoring network operations or developing the skills for detecting out-of-band activities in a network environment. But generally, when an "out of normal condition" develops, the Team should mobilize into action mode, to determine the cause of the abnormal traffic and structure appropriate reaction at all levels.

If one analyzes major criminal intrusion incidents (such as the major data breaches against retailers, banks, and other institutions holding large amounts of valuable data), most of these events have been detected by network traffic analysis. Network traffic analysis and detection is where the protection of the network meets incident response. Is there abnormal traffic, functions that should not be on the network, or traffic trying to exit the firewall? These are signs of events outside the normal course of operations for the organization.

It is important that network administrators, who are assigned the duties of monitoring the function and health of the network, raise the alarm the moment abnormal traffic events are first detected. It is certainly too late when an outside law enforcement agency contacts you saying that they think you have been hacked.

That will also be the moment when news media will be contacting individuals within the organization to ask embarrassing questions. The better prepared your personnel are to seize control of a criminal incident, the better your organization will be able to address the subsequent fallout.

In many instances, inadequately trained IT operations personnel have ignored the early warning signs of malware attacks or other abnormal behavior and simply allowed the attackers to continue their surveillance of the IT infrastructure and exfiltration of information. Immediate access to the Team could have significantly reduced the damage inflicted by such attacks.

Internal Misconduct by an Individual or Group (Whether Criminal or Not)

A common event that takes place in many organizations is what is known forensically as the insider attack. This is the scenario where an insider (employee or contractor) removes information from the organization for personal financial or other form of gain, or to deliberately damage the organization. Think of the employee removing trade secrets, intellectual property, customer and vendor lists, etc., for the purpose of starting a business competitor. Or the disgruntled employee tampering with the accuracy of financial or business development files. Or, of course, the embezzler.

After the Snowden incident inside the US government, organizations have on the whole become more aware of this type of incident. Still, many organizations do not know how to recognize and gather useful electronic information to investigate this type of event, either for civil lawsuit purposes or for criminal prosecution.

There is a risk of accusing good employees of something that they have not done, thereby losing employees loyalty, or even triggering a lawsuit for wrongful termination. In such cases, it is better for personnel who are trained in handling such incidents to conduct the investigations. In many cases organizations will hire an external third party with no interest in the dispute to collect and analyze information that may become evidence in court. A well-trained in-house Team will be prepared to recognize the scope of the situation and decide whether there is a need for outside investigation.

In most insider incidents it is common to place the suspect on paid administrative leave so that harm is kept to a minimum, both to the organization's assets and to its employee morale. It is easier to tell an employee that there is a problem and until it is sorted out he can remain at home for few days, rather than to terminate the person and then try to make amends when suspicions prove groundless.

Other Criminal Misconduct, Fraud, etc., by an Individual or Group

In some cases, fraud, harassment, and other actions involving the organization's computers may be criminal in nature. Once the crime is uncovered, it is important to immediately notify the law enforcement agency with jurisdiction over the matter, including asking for specific instructions about preserving evidence for the law enforcement investigation.

For example, while producing or possessing pornography of adults is not illegal in the United States, child pornography is. It must be reported immediately once it is discovered. In the adult case, it is a business policy offense. In the other case, it is a felony offense. Similarly, it is necessary to report incidents such as embezzlement, fraud, bribery, and other similar crimes directly and immediately to law enforcement. These are nonnegotiable, even though they bring outsiders into your computer system.

If anyone in management is in doubt, consult immediately with experienced legal counsel as to the local criminal laws and any applicable regulatory regime governing what your organization is required to do.

But before you can substantiate that a crime has been committed against or within your organization and needs to be reported, you need to immediately preserve possible evidence so that you can continue the internal investigation to determine the source and scope of the incident.

This is the moment for the Team leaders to remind everyone concerned: Do not assume. Preserve evidence and inquire.

There have been many incidents of an apparent criminal nature that on the surface appear to be committed by an insider. A wrong accusation is made due to malpractice on the part of the internal investigator, or there is a rush to judgment on the part of management. As the outcomes of those incidents show, it is a lot easier to fall into this hole through lack of reliable evidence than it is to climb out of it afterward.

Thus it is critical that all the facts are gathered and then confirmed via alternate methodologies to properly substantiate the allegations. When all the information is assembled and actual facts are confirmed, then decisions can be made. This does not mean that management should simply run with all accusations gathered in the first one hour of investigation.

A good example is an incident in which it appeared initially that an accountant had diverted funds to a personal account. But an in-depth investigation revealed that a third party, looking for a promotion, had logged in to the accountant's workstation while he was away from his desk to sabotage his career. Similar incidents have been noted where pornography was loaded into the victim's computer by an in-house competitor in an attempt to have the person terminated. Good evidence-gathering methodology is the key.

When Something is Wrong and the Origin is Unknown: Log Access is Critical

In cases where the specific nature and extent of an apparent intrusion event is not known, it is important to preserve as much information as possible from the affected workstations, servers, and other devices. This is because it is difficult on the initial assessment to determine precisely what the scope of the event was and precisely how it has developed.

This type of incident requires a coordinated team approach in order to quickly triage the systems and narrow down the point and type of attack without further impacting the organization. In these types of cases the analysis of logs and network traffic becomes imperative in determining where the root of the attack is located.

Without the log information it is almost impossible to conclusively find the source. This means that extensive techniques of individually examining many machines will need to be done.

Also, in these cases a Team that has been trained in preliminary examination of systems can help narrow the root of the attack in short order.

When Immediate Action is Needed

In certain types of incidents, such as when an unauthorized wire transfer is being executed by an external attacker, it is necessary for the Team to act swiftly and in a coordinated way. In such cases, evidence collection needs to be minimized temporarily so that immediate actions can be taken to prevent further loss.

What is necessary after that immediate protective action is to document the information that helped to determine the reason for such action, so that the Team responders can properly account for the action taken as they go forward to preserve evidence.

When Criminal or Civil Litigation is Likely: Expanding the Team as Needed

At the time a reasonable person would expect a specific criminal or civil trial, by events, words, threats, etc., it is a good time for the Team to begin thinking about what specific information is critical to respond to the incident now, and what information may later be needed as evidence at trial.

As an example, if the IT Security Manager or Chief Information Security Officer (CISO) receives a call from law enforcement that they suspect the company has been hacked, it is important to alert the Team and begin the investigation process, to determine if this is an ongoing event, and to outline its scope for response.

From the moment the incident is identified, the process of evidence preservation needs to be implemented to the extent of the best knowledge at hand. In many cases, this preservation blanket needs to be adjusted to accommodate new boundaries for the event and include previously unknown information. The Team should make reexamination of the entire scope of the incident and reevaluation of appropriate procedures a routine part of the ongoing preservation process.

At the same time legal, finance (if credit cards or bank accounts are involved), and other departments or personnel may need to be involved. Each should be investigating in their areas of expertise to determine the extent of the event, as well as which partners, suppliers, and customers need to be notified of the event. Emergency notifications may be appropriate if it appears the criminal incident may spread to others or have come through one of them.

This does not mean that anyone should notify the press with unsubstantiated information. But establishing the boundaries of the event needs to take place as quickly as possible so those boundaries can be transmitted to all necessary areas of management.

Once the extent of the event is determined, appropriate company-wide and public statements to be issued by management can be drafted, vetted by the Team for accuracy, and released to inform the community at large, as appropriate.

It should be made plain to everyone, from the very formation of the Team onward, that any unauthorized media contact will be considered a firing offense. An opportunity to hold forth in front of a reporter, especially with a cameraman, must be politely but firmly refused, regardless of begging, pleading, promises, etc. Silence by the Team must be absolute and permanent. In our opinion, a media leak is a separate problem of its own. A media leak from the Team is a disaster that could compromise the evidence that the Team is trying to preserve.

When Litigation is in Progress

If litigation, whether civil or criminal, is already in progress and the litigators receive a request for additional information that was not previously anticipated by the organization, then it is the Team's job to analyze the request and determine whether it is reasonable, if the information requested is in a form already preserved, and if there is available ESI sufficient to fulfill the request.

For example, there are litigators who are accustomed to only receiving information in a certain form, but they do not make that known during the preliminary (Rule 26) negotiations. Once they receive what you have provided, they request the same data, but in a different form, because they do not know how to handle information in your format. In such cases the requests can be declined by your counsel after conferring with the Team, with an explanation that all content requested has already been produced, although not in the manner that they expected, due to a lack of specificity in their initial request.

In other cases, the opposing lawyers will request the same data, but from other sources, and use that to leverage their request into expanded production of data beyond the scope of the case at hand. This is the discovery equivalent of fishing in the pond versus deep-sea fishing. It is still just fishing. Once again, this where the other Team members can assist the litigators on the Team, by explaining the possible reasons for expanding data preservation, or not doing so.

WHO NEEDS TO ACT: WHOEVER HANDLES THE PROBLEM IS ON THE TEAM

Information Technology Personnel

As the custodian of all stored ESI, the IT department is the obvious critical component in the evidence preservation and collection effort.

In order to achieve preservation effectively, the IT members of the Team need to be trained in basic preservation and collection techniques. No one should assume that those techniques would be part of the regular IT skill set.

If that precise technical knowledge is not present in your organization at the time of the criminal incident or civil triggering event, it is critical to immediately engage the services of an outside forensic IT consultant who has experience in this process. One cannot emphasize this enough. More mistakes are made in the initial preservation and collection part of the ESI processing due to technical ignorance than in any other component of the overall process. And obviously mistakes which destroy information at this early stage are the hardest to overcome.

The forensic IT consultant, if hired before the critical moment, needs to be an effective trainer, showing your Team's IT members how to act immediately and effectively in preserving digital information. If your Team's IT members are not yet trained in forensically-effective preservation techniques when an incident occurs, the outside forensic IT consultant must be a leader to the IT sub-team in order to get the preservation task done without delay, with more orderly training to follow.

What does the training entail? Here is a short list of some notable failures in the preservation process to think about:

- delaying the collection process longer than necessary;
- failing to stop reusing tapes on the backup rotation cycle;
- failing to back up email, database, and mobile device servers as soon as possible to prevent overwriting of data; and
- failing to preserve data contained in laptops, phones, portable storage drives, and other devices.

Think about the few events in this list. Then also think about the cost of trying to recover the same information after months or years have passed since the incident. The cost of recovery alone can be multiple times the original cost of a backup and some storage media.

Preservation and collection are not activities that can be learned out of a book alone. There are forensic protocol classes that train IT administrators and incident responders on live systems. In these classes, people are trained in laboratory conditions so that they go through the experience of encountering the many problems that different systems can present. Such classes, when taught by experienced and certified forensics trainers, are well worth the cost to the individual employees and to the organization.

Human Resources Personnel

In most incidents that have an identified individual as a component, it is prudent to include the HR department on the Team. This is particularly important any time there is an employee or captive contractor as witness, victim, suspect, or ESI custodian in the case.

In addition, HR is the repository of rules and policies that address the behavior of people in the organization. HR personnel are the ones who are going to help determine if those policies and rules have been violated and to what extent. They should participate, not just to take action, but also to help determine the extent to which the organization's own structure or policies may have contributed to the incident itself.

For example, an organization that lacks written policies about the use of personal computing devices on the organization's premises or involving the organization's information could be hard pressed later to make a case that the employee purposefully attempted to steal corporate data, especially if the suspect claims that it was an inadvertent mistake after they are caught. This has occurred in past incidents the authors have investigated, and the upshot has been this: if the policies and procedures are poorly designed, poorly implemented, or ignored all together, it is very difficult to make a case when the suspect is part of the organization to begin with.

Another example of HR's value on the Team is the problem of sharing of passwords because a supervisor is too busy or too lazy to log in and provide access necessary for the employee. Instead, the supervisor lets the employee use the admin user ID and password to get access to information. Is that a policy violation by an escalation of privileges? Not if the supervisor allowed it to happen.

Situations of these kinds are HR's natural territory, and you will probably want this expertise on the Team in most instances.

Financial Personnel

Most events that have concerned us as legal and forensic professionals have had a financial component. The event was related to money or property being taken, a loss of assets or business opportunities, insurance issues, or a financial penalty in some form. Financial personnel can quantify these losses, a calculation that is needed early in any litigation.

Additionally, the financial personnel will help quantify the costs of the incident itself. This will help legal counsel establish proportionality with respect to the collection and preservation components of the response. Proportionality, as you remember, is the balance between what is lost and the cost of the evidence to prove it. It should not cost $500,000 to get to trial on a $500,000 loss. Financial personnel can help the lawyers shape a proportional evidence-discovery strategy. They can also help to craft a response to unfounded objections from opposing counsel about the cost of preserving ESI.

If the incident is of a financial nature (eg, a data breach with credit card data involved), it is critical to involve the financial personnel because this a federal crime. There are thresholds that are triggered at various levels of money stolen or otherwise compromised in a criminal incident. You are not just required to alert law enforcement, but there are also regulatory requirements to alert various agencies having oversight over the industry or the organization itself.

Finally, the cost of responding to the incident itself needs to be estimated and allocated for financial reporting purposes. No one but the financial members of the Team should even want to get near this part of the effort.

Other Management Personnel

Most incident-response Teams have links to the tiers of management that must be alerted to any incident (assuming the alert didn't come from management in the first place). The Team needs to know what level of management must be included in its decision-making, and what levels kept advised, as the severity of the incident and dollar value escalates.

In addition, depending on the size and complexity of your organization, departmental and/or divisional management issues may dictate that additional management areas be either included directly on the Team or kept closely in the loop as the Team's evidence preservation proceeds. But remember, the Team is designed to be a directly-engaged working group, not a management policy group. Only the rolled-up sleeves belong at this table.

In today's world of Twitter, Facebook, and other social media, there are few secrets that stay secret. It is unwise to have a Team policy of obfuscation that could expose senior management and the reputation of the organization itself to embarrassment, ridicule and the anger of the consuming public and their own customers. Take note of the media and market reactions to several major companies that waited weeks or months to notify their customers of a data breach. You can never win the secrets game.

In many cases a senior level manger or a midlevel manager who has regular access to senior management "heads" the Team, in terms of official Team structure. There will be many circumstances in which other Team members should temporarily lead the Team, or subgroups of the Team, especially when several tasks must be accomplished simultaneously.

The overall Team leader, regardless of job title, must be a person who respects the skill sets brought to the table by each of the other individuals (and their back-up members) on the Team.

The leader must also be someone who can avoid "mission creep" and maintain the Team's focus on evidence preservation in the course of reacting to the other developing elements of the incident. Remind people, this is an evidence Team not a crisis management Team. You should not be carrying the load for other management functions.

You don't need a Senior Executive VP leading the Team. But management needs to know at all times what the Team is up to, and have confidence in the Team's structure on a continuing basis. If an incident is sufficiently complex, co-leaders may be needed, to be certain the upward information flow is properly maintained while all the Team members are planning, acting, reporting in, and considering. It is also useful to reconsider the leadership structure as an event progresses, for the same reasons.

The whole purpose of the Team, and for its evidence preservation protocol, is so that management knows, when push comes to shove, that there is reliable, admissible evidence to back up management's position at the negotiating table or in the courtroom. If management is not supremely confident in the Team, everyone is in trouble.

The Lawyers
In-House Counsel Team—Lawyers Plus Paralegals
It is obvious that the corporate legal group is a major part of the Team. They assess the incident from a legal perspective and help decide the points at which to alert outside counsel and other management layers as the situation develops. The regulatory compliance group (assuming they are associated with your legal department) also needs to be kept in the loop. Just like the IT personnel, it is necessary for your in-house lawyers to be part of the Team's process from hour one.

In organizations that do not have an internal legal counsel, or where all litigation issues are outsourced, a member of management who regularly interacts with outside litigation counsel needs to be active on the Team. This management member of the Team serves as the link to the organization's litigators to get legal advice on the seriousness of the case and the evidence issues as the facts unfold.

The main point is that you cannot ignore the importance of having attorneys and their trained staff as active Team members to provide various assessments of the event as it takes place or is recognized, and as things move forward toward resolution.

In addition, Team members need to recognize the skill set of paralegal assistants in developing the lists of types of information for preservation, recognizing certain kinds of information as likely evidence, maintaining the critical "we have/we don't have" lists, and organizing quantities of evidence in the forms needed by the attorneys in pretrial discovery and at trial. These individuals can be the Team's true workhorses if their skills are properly recognized and assigned.

Litigation Counsel Team—Lawyers Plus Paralegals

If your organization has an inside legal department without its own litigators, it is your outside legal team that typically will handle litigation preparation. In such cases the lead outside counsel is responsible for all communication with the opposing side, for negotiations for the initial conference between the opposing sides (under Federal Rule 26) and for developing and executing the discovery plan—both requesting information and organizing information for delivery to the opposing side.

It is critical that the litigators on the Team be kept apprised of all issues regarding digital evidence collection, preservation and analysis, as someone else in the legal department is attending to paper evidence collection and review. The digital evidence issues include the existence and condition of legacy computer systems (systems that have been replaced but still contain ESI), identification of all sources of ESI for preservation, and other issues and unplanned events that could jeopardize the production of ESI in the course of the litigation. The lawyer may well ask for "all documents" but every Team member needs to know that such a request includes electronic documents at numerous locations as well as the contents of physical file drawers.

It is also important to note that if litigation counsel shows a lack of interest in or attention to the issues of ESI preservation and the Rule 26 process, as it relates to digital evidence processing, that attitude could place the organization's chances of success in jeopardy. This is not the proper century for lawyers to think of documents as pieces of paper or to be ignorant of the technical details of ESI production. The 2015 amendments to the Rules make this abundantly plain. We are not saying that your Team's senior litigators with years of strategic expertise should be unwelcome, just that there should be technically competent litigators actively at work on the Team to handle the practical details of the electronic evidence process. The Team's focus is evidence, not trial strategy.

The Digital Forensic Expert or Consultant

If you are the person designated as the Team's in-house digital forensic expert or its outside digital forensic consultant, then it is part of your task to go into action whenever there is an incident (in civil matters, a triggering event) requiring a litigation hold.

Initially, when you receive information that a litigation hold notice is going to go out to the organization, your duties include developing appropriate technical details for the hold notice, so that every individual within the organization will know exactly what to do (and not do) if they are in contact in any way with ESI that needs preservation.

You also will be developing and disseminating the technical details of a preservation strategy to isolate the appropriate electronic data with the least amount of disruption to the day-to-day operations of the organization, using the tools you have previously installed and tested for this particular organization.

Generally, organizations that have a Team with an in-house digital forensics expert will have applications like FTK Enterprise or Encase Enterprise to conduct the collection process from the various custodians. (Note: These products are named solely as examples. We do not endorse any product for any purpose. We just want you to be aware that such products exist.)

If on the other hand, you are an outside consultant, but you have been previously retained to train and support the internal Team, you should have already developed a strategy for this particular client. This would include working with your contact person on the Team, to have in place prior to an incident all of the tools, specialized workstations, and any other special arrangements you will need when the moment comes.

In cases where you receive a call from a new client, you will need to survey the digital environment, and develop a strategy on the fly to do the best possible job of preserving the ESI related to the case. It is common in these circumstances that there is a tendency to over-collect ESI due to the potential for missing a key component of the evidence. For example this is usually the scenario where 150 desktop computers are imaged in their entirety simply because there are no tools already installed in the network to parse the data files by date, subject, or other parameters. There are many other examples where the cost of collection can be four to five times the cost of a planned collection strategy under these "failure to plan" circumstances.

We hope you as a consultant are simultaneously advocating for the Team to be organized as you work. Meanwhile, wait for someone to surprise you by casually mentioning in passing the "old" system, in which they can find what you want a lot faster.

Other Expert Consultants and Expert Witnesses

Keep in mind that depending on the nature and scope of the incident, the Team may need to coordinate with or provide data for specialized experts in other fields. These experts will have unique data requirements in order to render an opinion, and their data will need to be collected and preserved in a manner similar to the well-executed litigation hold process.

It is important that the Team should know the specific requirements of those other experts as soon as each expert is determined to be necessary, so that the data can be preserved and collected before its destruction becomes probable.

For example, an 18-wheeler accident will require the collection of the data from the navigation computer in the tractor in order to account for the driver's actions prior to the accident. Preservation and collection of that kind of evidence should never be delegated to someone who is not knowledgeable about that esoteric form of ESI storage.

Experienced litigators and your in-house counsel should already have, or be able to prepare quickly, lists of specialized information needed for different types of predictable events involving all the usual personal and corporate disasters. Your organization's insurance advisers are an excellent source of guiding statistics for identifying these likely incidents. They may even have a list or two at hand, just waiting for management to ask.

PREPARING THE TEAM

Planning—Prepare the Team for Various Situations Before Anything Happens

As we have mentioned, the need for planning and training cannot be emphasized enough. While you have the leisure to think clearly you should identify the appropriate Team slots, and which individuals have the skill sets to fill those slots for different kinds of events. The time to do this is not when a major incident is in progress, and people are (metaphorically) running around screaming and waving their hands in the air, but in advance of any incident.

There are litigation support consultants, similar to disaster recovery planning consultants, who will help an organization to develop Team plans and identify individuals who should be on the Team for various types of circumstances.

Critically, the consultant needs to understand that you want the Team to consist of the people with the absolute best skill sets for each kind of event, not the people with the most important job titles. Being appointed to this group should be a summons to hard work under bad circumstances, not just an honor to go on the employee's resume.

The consultant should also identify back-up members for each Team position in case a designated member moves on or is otherwise unavailable when the incident occurs. A critical Team member who is on a hiking vacation in rural Newfoundland is not going to be useful, but a fully trained back-up person can save the day, thanks to good planning.

The consultant can then assess the strengths and needs of the Team, and its members' individual needs for training, including forensic and ESI preservation training.

The consultant can also prepare plans for the designated Team members to practice working together. The training needs to include not only opportunities for Team members to learn their own roles, but also tabletop exercises to develop the necessary group skills and appropriate group reactions, so all Team members are knowledgeable about how to share responsibility for a real incident. Seek a consultant in advance of placing the Team in action, to help you develop these strategies and roles, and to provide the necessary training for your Team members' specific needs.

Identifying Key Team Positions for Various Situations

Every position on the Team is not required to be involved in every instance. Certain types of incidents can be focused enough that some Team members can be excused from participating.

Indeed, as your Team grows in experience and confidence, a smaller group may be as effective as the initial larger Team. Some former members may "graduate" to become Team resources, whose Team experience gives them the ability to answer the Team's questions easily on an instant's notice.

But in almost every instance your Team will need legal, IT, and the forensic expert.

Training Individuals for Team Positions (Including Their Support Staff)

General training for a Team position is not litigation-support training or forensic training. We are not saying that every Team member needs to have an in-depth knowledge of legal procedure or the forensic process.

However, all Team members should have a general overview of the forensic process so that they understand the hurdles and obstacles encountered in the collection, preservation and analysis process, as well as the larger litigation picture. With a minimum of focused training, each individual can adequately function within the Team as well as responding as needed to inquiries from their own supervisors.

This pre-event training will also avoid the additional stresses of bringing individuals with no knowledge of either forensics or the litigation process up to speed in the middle of a crisis.

We do recommend that each Team member's support staff be given a brief introduction to the Team's function and their own Team member's specific assignment, so that routine matters can briefly be handed off if necessary, if the event expands in unexpected ways. An email bulletin to other Team members does not have to come from the Team member's own hands if a support staff member is able to competently pass the message along and free up the Team member for more skilled efforts.

Pre-Crisis Forensic and Litigation Training—The Heart of a Successful Team

Identifying the types of incidents that repeat themselves in a particular organization will help develop the Team's responses, so dealing with those kinds of incidents becomes less stressful and more confidence-inspiring for the entire organization.

One way of developing the response scenarios in Fortune 500 companies is to analyze the litigation and insurance-claim history of the company, identifying cases by their triggers to categorize them properly. For example, the 18-wheeler accident would require that a representative from the transportation group be on the Team, so that issues related not only to obvious safe driving questions but also to environmental compliance, driver regulations, etc. can be promptly identified and evidence adequately preserved. This expedites regulatory as well as litigation responses.

Once the frequent types of incidents are identified, you can develop the strategic items that will be critical to minimize the loss from the incident while preserving data that will support that strategy in the event of litigation. It is this information that is used to develop the team-training model and strategies.

Identifying Outside Training Consultants, Especially the Forensic Consultant

The selection of training consultants is important. You need to select an individual who has hands-on experience in the field in which he or she is training your Team. This is not a theory class, but a practical application of what is taught in the classroom. It is important that the individual trainer is capable of communicating exactly how to execute the necessary strategies, and how to develop flexibility in those strategies that can be carried out by the Team in the heat of the crisis, using the tools that have already been installed to support them. Theory is nice, but detailed practical advice in an appropriate context is key.

Dedicated Internal Forensic Teams—Advantages and Disadvantages

If your organization can afford to develop an internal forensics group within the Team, you will be able to optimize your preservation, collection and examination processes, thus maximizing your savings. One of the author's clients has achieved as much as a 60% savings over the cost of having outside consultants doing the same work that their internal team is able to achieve, and has done this over eight consecutive years.

It is a major advantage because management can have access to the process on an ongoing basis, and can adjust the strategy for each case as it develops and as the Team discovers information.

On the other hand, the costs associated with establishing an internal forensic team are high, from the laboratory equipment, to training, licensing, and insurance. Getting started can appear daunting to a mid-size organization. Long-term considerations of many kinds, as well as start-up costs, need to be part of the analysis.

Making Sure Everyone Knows Who's Going To Do What in Various Situations
Team Members

It is important that both in-house and external Team members know their own roles and responsibilities, as well as those of all the other Team members, in advance of the incident. This results from training plus exercises, such as reviewing the execution of the hold process in prior cases.

With individual training and teamwork in place, the Team can execute the preservation plan set out in the litigation hold notice with a minimal amount of wasted effort by the Team members as well as disruption to the organization.

Everyone Else

Besides training your organization's Team, it is important that you provide practical information about the Team's existence to all employees, with appropriate training about how the Team is activated and how employees and contractors interface with Team members in various situations. Each individual employee and contractor must know about their own place in the entire litigation hold process, so as to avoid the dreaded "guess what I did" by an overly helpful but unskilled employee.

For example, all employees and contractors need to know how to recognize and properly report a triggering event or incident, and how to see that critical information gets passed promptly to the appropriate level within the organization.

Each individual should also know whom to contact with questions about a preservation letter or litigation hold notice or memo, if they do not understand some part of it.

All members of the organization also need to know what to do about information in nonobvious locations—stored at the department level, in offsite computers or storage devices disconnected from the network, in the "Cloud," in the hands for former holders of a position, etc. Litigators have had major surprises in the courtroom when they have called a witness to testify, and as part of that process the witness is asked to bring with them any and all information they have in their possession or control related to the litigation. It will be extremely difficult to recover one's positive momentum during the trial if the witness appears with a USB device that has files the litigation team did not previously know about.

This is a situation in which HR personnel are critical, guaranteeing that the support staff associated with a key player (especially a former employee) are identified and contacted at the beginning of the process. In addition, HR can quickly and efficiently determine, whether personal devices are used by key players (whether or not such a policy is in place), so that relevant ESI on those devices can be secured. This is particularly critical for organizations that have "BYOD" (Bring Your Own Device) policies, about which we will have more to say later.

When clear policies and procedures about ESI are in place, enforced, and routinely refreshed in personnel training, the Team's job of preserving digital evidence will be concluded quickly and efficiently with minimal disruption to regular business, and with minimal chances of The Big Surprise in settlement negotiations or in the courtroom.

That of course is your goal and ours—for your organization to continue running smoothly, with business as usual, while the Team is doing amazing things with electronic evidence.

CHAPTER 4

Understanding Information Systems

INTRODUCTION TO THE DIGITAL FORENSIC WORLD

The next several chapters (Chapters 4–9) cover the digital forensics topics of how to understand what you have, why the proper procedure in collection of information is important to a case, how the information needs to be collected, from what sources, and how to do so in a cost-effective manner. This information will not make you an expert on the subject of digital evidence collection and preservation. But, it will inform you so that better communication takes place between the forensic/IT Team members, attorneys on the Team, and management.

You can use this section as a reference to gain a capsule understanding of what underlying technology is applicable to the case at hand and the preservation issues involving the technology as presently implemented.

In today's world almost every lawsuit, criminal incident, or regulatory investigation has a digital component to its evidence. The computing device is either a direct tool of the disputed activity (such as removing the company's trade secrets to start a competing business) or the source of information about the activity (such as email discussions with others about excuses to terminate an inconvenient employee).

So why should an attorney, HR director, regulatory compliance officer, or mid-level manager understand the place of information systems in litigation? Because the Federal Rules of Civil Procedure (the Rules) require that the attorney must understand the IT particulars, and use them effectively, in order to successfully represent your organization's interests (Rule 26(f)(3)). The trial attorney will need the entire rest of the Team to do that effectively.

This does not mean that each Team member will need a degree in information science to be able to represent the organization's interests as either its lawyer, its litigation/risk manager, or as evidence custodian/witness. You just need a point of reference and source of information in order to understand the key components of information systems so you will be able to understand what your own teammates and the opposing side are saying to you. The next several

CONTENTS

(Continued)
55

chapters provide the knowledge for you to recognize when to have an expert in information systems by your side, guiding your hand (and mouth) to avoid digital disasters.

Information science has advanced significantly in the last 40 years. Much of the change has occurred in the power and miniaturization of the hardware and the simplification and modularization of the software.

There are many different types of information systems. This chapter covers the major types, but is not an all-inclusive source of every available type. It is designed to serve as a reference to the major components of information systems in the early 21st century. These components will change as the years go by, so the reader needs to understand that the advances will occur as time passes and changing techniques will be applied from different perspectives.

COMPUTER SYSTEMS

This chapter covers the types of computer systems that organizations and individuals commonly use today and those that are still in use from past generations. The chapter is divided into personal or stand-alone computers, network computers, servers, firewalls, and security devices. Each section will discuss the key components, and things to look for or ask about from the owner or user of the device, regarding its use, maintenance, and other aspects which are necessary to know in order to effectively collect its information in a forensically sound manner.

STAND-ALONE COMPUTERS

The realm of stand-alone computers (better known as personal computers) covers a large universe of products from lightweight tablets to workstations with over 32 processors. Today, these devices are many times more powerful than the mainframes that filled multiple rooms in the early 1970s. The computing industry has placed more computing power in the hands of the individual than anything anyone could have dreamed of 30 years ago.

So, what are the components of a computer, how do they work together to deliver information to the user, and what are the important components when there is an investigation and evidence needs to be collected?

Computer Architecture
The architecture of all computers is made up of various principal components that when brought together constitute a working computer. They include: the processor (interprets programs into actions), memory (stores information in real time while that information is being actively processed), permanent

storage (stores information, programs, and other instructions for long term use), and logic-boards (handle the communications, input, and output of the machine). There will also be an input device such as a keyboard and a visual interface such as a monitor or other screen. It will also have an output function.

Here is a diagram of the flow of information among the components:

$$INPUT \rightarrow PROCESSOR \rightarrow OUTPUT$$
$$| \qquad \qquad |$$
$$IN \quad OUT$$
$$| \qquad \qquad |$$
$$STORAGE$$

Of course this is a very basic representation of the many circuit boards and components that make the computer work, but it illustrates the principal components that every computer must have in order to be a computer.

In the beginning, the modern computer began as a hobby device in the 1970s with the development of build-it-yourself computers like the Altair 8080 and similar devices. These machines helped to develop the early operating systems, and guided the likes of Bill Gates and Steve Jobs to develop the first commercial systems to be implemented in offices and classrooms. These systems were simple and consisted of a keyboard, screen, printer, and computer board in a case.

Later, the introduction of the floppy drive added the capability of storing programs and information files that could be loaded by reading the media (floppy disk). Once this concept appeared, the adoption of computers into every organization was only a matter of time and money.

Evidence in Computers

There are very few jobs today that do not involve the use of a computer to at least some degree. Based on this, there are very few legal cases that can be identified as not involving a computer in some form or another.

An example is a robbery at a gas station. One would think that it involves people, a weapon, and the taking of money from the register. But it is not that simple. Most gas stations today have electronic safes that are wired to the alarm system, cameras that record patron and employee movements, and other sensor devices. In this case, gathering evidence would involve collecting the recorded camera feeds for the time period of the incident based on the electronic alarm system alerts, the electronic cash register logs, and any other relevant electronic information that can assist in the capture of the perpetrators. Similarly, this applies to just about every situation in today's ordinary life.

Yet, I as a digital forensics expert find it amusing that many attorneys in the 21st century can state with a straight face to a judge that there is no electronic evidence as part of their case. Now, on the other hand, one can reasonably say that there are cases that do not require the presentation of electronic evidence as part of the resolution process of the case. But it is advisable for counsel to acknowledge its existence and state that the electronic evidence does not add any value to the other available evidence demonstrating the facts of the case, rather than simply to ignore the existence and examination of digital evidence.

I have witnessed cases involving accounting, safety, inventory, insurance, and other areas where attorneys completely ignored the existence of electronic or computer-based evidence because they did not want to deal with it. As a reasonable person would suspect, things did not usually go well for those attorneys, unless the opposing attorney had the same attitude toward digital evidence and the judge did not care.

Collecting from Personal Computers

Law enforcement agencies are some of the most efficient collectors of computer evidence in the United States today. Due to extensive training, practice, and research they have honed the skills of evidence collection to a fine art, and developed the practices that exist today across all segments of the industry. The Scientific Working Group on Digital Evidence (SWGDE) was founded in 1992 by a group of government agents. It continues to this day, developing updated standards in the collection and handling of digital evidence. This author is proud to be a member of SWGDE and to be a contributor to the expansion of knowledge necessary to handle the expanding realm of digital evidence.

The collection of evidence from personal computers is the simplest type of collection in the realm of digital evidence. The types of evidence in a personal computer are: the content of the screen, the content of the memory (if the system is turned on), the hard disk, and any removable storage devices (memory sticks, external hard drives, disks associated with legacy systems, etc.) attached to the computer.

There are protocols for the order in which these types of storage are to be collected, based on their volatility and potential for loss of information. For example, in cases where the possibility of hacking is suspected, it is necessary to collect memory information first, to examine it for the possible existence of malware (software intended to act maliciously without the knowledge of the computer operator). In simpler cases like email harassment and the possibility of pornography, it is not as important to collect the memory of the computer's own recent functional activities.

Nevertheless, computer evidence, unlike wine, does not get better with age. It is critical that the collection process be implemented as soon as practical to eliminate the possibility of data loss from continued activity.

It is important that the digital evidence consultant (whether in-house or brought in for the occasion) understands the nature of the legal dispute, to be able to identify the sources where the relevant evidence is located.

Of course, for those readers who like to pay by the Gigabyte to collect information and think about its significance later, you can simply let the consultant collect as much information as the consultant feels is adequate. The consultant with only the haziest notion of what is in dispute will either just "sample" here and there in the designated computer, then wait for further instructions, or vastly over-collect out of professional paranoia. You, as a member of a trained incident-response Team, should not find either of those approaches very attractive.

Collected ESI Preservation

When working with stand-alone computers, the process of preserving the evidence is relatively straightforward. The hard drive must be imaged (a process sometimes referred to as "ghosting") to assure that there is a read-only copy supported by a mathematical hash or algorithm. The volatile content must also be downloaded and hashed with a validated forensic tool.

If the computer needs to be returned to production immediately, additional copies of the image and volatile content need to be made, in order to have some redundancy in case of mechanical failure. It is not necessary to retain the whole stand-alone computer system, screen, motherboard and processor section until the end of the litigation.

In a criminal case, there may be other reasons why keeping all the seized evidence is necessary, because they may contain other physical evidence such as fingerprints, DNA or other genetic factors, or evidence of tampering with the components, such as switching out a hard disk or use of unauthorized software.

Electronic evidence is highly fragile and rapidly perishable. When cases take a long time to get to trial and even longer when moving through the appeals process, it is important that the evidence drives are checked periodically by forensically trained personnel to prevent an evidence drive failure. Generally, it is my practice to use new drives for evidence preservation to prevent the possibility of a drive failure. I have seen cases where the opposing consultant arrives at the electronic evidence analysis lab only to discover that the evidence drive has failed, and it is necessary to retrieve either a copy or the original drives from the safe in order to make new images of the evidence. If the originals were released back into production, this could be an embarrassing moment, to say the least.

Best Practices for Data Collection

There are a number of national and international standards that outline the best practices for data collection of individual computers. The digital forensics industry as a whole tries to develop and update practices as new equipment and operating systems emerge.

In the United States, SWGDE, the American Society for Testing and Materials (ASTM) and the National Institute of Standards and Technology (NIST) are currently disseminating the best practices standards in the area of digital forensics. These bodies engage practitioners, academics, and government representatives in developing and updating the practice guidelines for the industry to follow. Their information can be found at various web sites that allow purchasing (in the case of ASTM) or free downloading of the various documents developed and published by each group.

Your digital forensics consultant will be able to tell you which organization's best practices he or she routinely uses.

NETWORKED COMPUTERS

This section covers groups of computers that are interconnected so as to operate together. Included here are all multi-unit systems, from the complex networks of large organizations to those in your home, if you are using the services of one of the large Internet service providers. For example, if you use a cable TV provider, they not only provide the Internet connection but also provide a wireless router that connects all devices in your home to that Internet connection. In the same manner, business systems are connected together by either wireless or wired connections, between offices, regions, and continents.

It is important to understand that these computer environments have the ability to transfer information easily between devices that may be geographically distant and to replicate information in multiple locations for the ease of users. For example, files or databases that are referenced frequently by a business may have multiple copies in different regions, so that the user or customer does not experience a "slow response" when accessing them.

It is in these cases that the consultant can develop strategies that reduce costs, find deleted information, or make a complicated problem simpler.

Networks can be characterized into two major types, local area networks and wide area networks.

In local area networks, the machines are connected via a switch or switches (dependent on the number of machines) and in turn connected to the Internet via an electronic gateway of some type. The most common in use today is a firewall in the form of an appliance (for example, brands such as Cisco, Fortinet, McAfee, WatchGuard, NetGear, SonicWall, etc. sell such physical devices). The purpose of the firewall is to separate and filter the outside network traffic from the inside network traffic and, in the process, limit what type of outside traffic comes into the private network.

Wide area networks connect over private circuits or the Internet among multiple locations of an organization, using encrypted digital tunnels to connect them together. In this case, firewalls are also used to provide access to the Internet and to remote company assets at other locations via the tunnels. In such cases, you have the ability for servers to synchronize content for ease of use and disaster recovery procedures.

Again, the structure of the local or wide area network can work to the digital consultant's advantage in developing time- and cost-saving strategies for evidence collection and preservation.

Disaster Recovery and Continuity of Operations

The purpose of disaster recovery and continuity of operations preparation is to keep the business going when conditions disrupt the normal operations of the business functions and services. Included in this group of functions is the IT function and its supporting operations. The reason why it is important to look at these procedures is because they can be valuable in finding information that may be stored long after the data in the primary location has been deleted or modified.

For example, backup tapes are frequently used to find the files that have been modified multiple times over a period of time, or deleted emails that have been pruned from the email server. In those cases, it can be more efficient to find that backup tape, hard disk, or whatever other media was used as part of the disaster recovery and continuity of operations routine, and recover the content needed from it.

Database Replication

A large part of the information stored in major organizations is stored in databases. Databases are very efficient engines to retrieve, index and update information. If you think of all the records that describe a person today, the majority of that information is stored in various databases.

Most databases today are designed using the relational model. This model uses data dictionaries to describe the elements of the data, and reuses the information as much as possible.

Another feature of databases is that they are designed to allow for the recovery of information using database logs and regular backups.

Finally, these features are combined to have effective replication scenarios that allow a master database to be replicated (copied) to multiple locations and instances, which will allow the data to be examined by large numbers of users.

These conditions and setups allow for the collection of information based on a number of variables, such as time zones, work hours, etc.

Automated Replication

Automated replication is the concept of copying files across multiple data centers, for the purpose of making the files available to users at multiple locations, allowing faster access for all users.

In many ways this is one of the primary purposes for the currently popular cloud computing. There are also services that allow for the concurrent modification of a file from multiple locations.

The bottom line for this function is to have the most current information visible to everyone interested in the data.

Network Metadata

Networks themselves generate information about the files on the network. This information, metadata, can be used to determine what, when, and by whom a file has been created and modified in a stored location.

This can be critical when the question is when someone knew what information was available, or what workstation made changes to the information in the file.

This type of information can also establish timelines of events that occurred in a system. Every file has a certain amount of file metadata associated with it, some more than others, based on the software that creates the file.

It is important that when negotiations take place between the sides to a dispute on the methods used to collect and produce data from information systems, that the process used for data collection does not destroy that metadata. For example, the delivery of emails in TIFF format removes the creation and modification metadata hidden in the email data, providing only the visible content of the document. If you are absolutely positive that is all you want, no problem. But know what you are agreeing to.

Network Device Log Information

The collection of network device logs has rapidly increased in importance with the emergence of data breach investigations. When properly configured, networks collect information on the activities that are occurring in the network at all times. When collected and analyzed against each other, these log files can reveal valuable information about the events leading to the network attack and data theft.

The key is that the log information has to be collected in a contemporaneous manner, since most network devices lack large amounts of data storage space.

Most well-designed networks will have a dedicated log server to collect the information generated by switches, routers, firewalls, and other devices that manage network traffic. These logs will have the information that answers the what, when, and who accessed, changed, or attacked the network and what servers they accessed.

SERVERS

The world of servers is little understood outside of the IT world. Most outsiders view them as the proverbial repository of knowledge or as the center of all information. These descriptions are not very accurate or helpful in many ways. But servers do store large amounts of information as well as distribute and share it, so that the server enables the system's users to work more efficiently.

Servers come in all sizes, from something as small as a desktop computer with server software installed in it, to large mainframes that handle very large databases and that store things like multi-branch bank account information, airline reservations and other large repositories of data.

One can view a server as a shared computer that enables two or more people to share files with each other and also allows others to have access to the information. This access is granted via permissions, and is controlled by the use of user accounts and passwords.

In the early days of servers, users' computers were hard-wired to the server by electrical conductors of various types. Today, users can access servers using wired and wireless technologies that allow for access from multiple locations and across continents using the Internet as the transport medium.

Also, a brief glance at the apps on your mobile phone shows that devices that are not computers can access servers.

Small Enterprise Servers

A server is actually a specialized piece of software that provides "services" to users requesting those services. Most people associate the "server" with a computer in a box, because that is the manner in which servers appear to their users in most day-to-day applications.

But given today's computing power, personal computers can also contain elements of servers by installing software that can perform the task. Most small businesses rely on one or more servers to accomplish the daily tasks of communications, file storage, and data processing. In the case of very small businesses, this can all be done in one box that provides server services of various kinds. For example, Microsoft has a family of small business servers that combine multiple functions in one box.

In situations where the client is a small organization, the level of technical skills of on-site employees tasked with the IT function may be quite limited. The small organization may even be totally reliant on an outside contractor who provides routine, limited IT maintenance services. This person may be perfectly capable of conducting maintenance tasks (the usual job), but utterly unqualified to conduct a data collection that is forensically sound. In such cases, it may be advantageous to hire the services of a digital forensics consultant with the necessary skills to assess, collect and filter the digital evidence in accordance with the requirements of the case. A specific inquiry about the inside IT employee or outside IT contractor's digital forensic skill certifications would be appropriate before a triggering event makes it an issue.

There are many examples in legal cases of small businesses trying to do this process by themselves and ending in major disasters. A case that comes to mind is *Victor Stanley, Inc. v. Creative Pipe, Inc.* (269 F.R.D. 497 (D. Md. 2010), citing *The Sedona Conference Commentary on Legal Holds: The Trigger and the Process*), where the owner of one of the parties conducted his own unskilled and disastrous "collection" of digital evidence, resulting in a determination of evidence spoliation. He eventually ended up losing the case after substantial monetary sanctions.

Server Groups and Enterprise Computing

In medium-sized companies workstations, servers, and other devices are managed and maintained by a trained IT group or department with skills to operate the equipment and support the user community. Companies such as these still need the assistance of a consultant, due to forensic skill shortages, but the internal IT personnel are not required to be walked through every step down the path to complete all the preliminary tasks necessary for conducting a data collection.

Such trained (but not forensics-specialized) personnel are excellent managers of server groups. Server groups are assembled together by networking various types of servers to provide a number of services to the client computers. They can be clustered to provide redundancy and failover functionality.

In these types of environment, the consultant can provide strategies that can simplify the evidence collection process by limiting the amount of data collected and processed as evidence. Additionally, the consultant can develop strategies to collect data with minimal disruption to business operations.

Distributed Computing

Most distributed computing environments tend to appear in larger organizations, where multiple servers are located in equipment rooms at multiple locations. These environments serve in some cases as a failover location for another data center and can have data duplicates that, if collected, are of little value. In these cases, it is important that the consultant sits down with the client and understands the specific uses of each location, as well as exact differences between data centers, and the reasons for their existence.

Mainframes and Large Scale Systems

Organizations that operate large-scale computing environments tend to be very large business operations. They generally have very competent information systems divisions. These personnel are capable of conducting their own collections and understand the process quite well. In these cases, the role of the consultant is more as an advisor to the client in developing strategies for the particular circumstances developing out of the triggering event.

FIREWALLS AND SECURITY DEVICES

For a long time network devices, the equipment that ran the network, had little forensic information associated with them. Part of this was because the devices had very small amounts of working memory, and most of it was dedicated to making the device work.

In the past 15 years, these devices have developed many capabilities. The new capabilities includes the ability to store information that can include metadata. That network-device metadata could provide clues as to what occurred in the network. Properly configured, the network devices can provide a highly informative map, using log information on how employees or intruders accessed a network and servers. This will show the spread of viruses and other malware that is/was inside.

Proper forensic preservation of the network metadata can give evidence as well as information pinpointing data destruction or transfers of information to an unauthorized site. When the investigation leads to the possibility of deliberate destruction or removal of sensitive information, the forensically preserved network metadata can hold a wealth of information. This will point in many cases to the perpetrators.

Routers and Firewalls

The name "Cisco" is synonymous with the word "router" for IT experts. The company essentially commercialized the devices that guide traffic over networks on a worldwide basis. There are many other manufacturers of routers, but the basic principles of routing data around networks remains the same, regardless of brand.

A router is a device that directs the data packets (file pieces) where they are destined, whether the Internet, a server, or some other device that stores or processes data. Most routers produce log information that collects configuration, traffic, and errors in the network as that information passes via the router to another network. This information can be used to trace network traffic and decode files sent over the network.

Similarly, firewalls are specialized routers with extended capabilities that allow for the inspection of network traffic before it enters or leaves a network en route to another network over the Internet or through a private connection. Firewalls are specifically designed to generate extensive logs. This allows for the recording of detailed information, including the origin and destination of data streams passing through the device.

The transfer of confidential information from a server to an outside storage device can illustrate how data from these types of devices is used. The transfer of the file will be recorded in the router and firewall logs, with time stamps and connection information, including the originating workstation identification that initiated the transfer of data. It was in a case like this that one of the authors found a repository for patient information of a large hospital chain, being stored and offered for sale to identity thieves.

Switch Traffic and Logs

The information received from network switches is similar to that of routers and firewalls. But this information gives alerts of attempted connection by unauthorized network devices seeking the internal network of the organization. In many cases, insiders attempting to hack an organization from within will bring a small device to work that they try to connect to the network, to gain access while bypassing the routers and firewalls set to prevent external attacks.

Administrative Logs

The network's administrative logs are important because they record how users are logged in to the network, whether locally or remotely. These administrative logs also record any attempts to use unauthorized passwords to access information from the organization. When combined with the logs of routers, firewalls, and switches, these administrative logs create a blueprint, which determines the origin of an attack and what types of information have been taken.

Log Aggregation Tools

The use of log aggregation tools is critical in the analysis of network metadata. The tools enable matching that can make sense of the network traffic in an efficient and effective manner. Without these types of tools, it would be a very time-consuming, and probably unreliable, task to create the connections between various events at separate devices to determine what occurred on the network during a certain time period.

With information about the structure and uses of your own system, your Team will be able to identify the kinds of forensic activity you will need to accomplish. Then you can identify the specific skills your Team needs.

CHAPTER 5

In Addition to the System—Other Devices

This chapter explains the difference between computer systems and the avalanche of mobile devices being introduced into the consumer and business markets in the past few years. We also raise some concerns about how these devices are being used in the business context, notably BYOD.

MOBILE DEVICES

The proliferation of personal smart phones and tablets is alone an overwhelming challenge in the field of digital forensics.

When the array of other mobile devices and applications being introduced today is added to it, with a multitude of operating systems and communication variants, the forensics expert faces a serious challenge in effectively collecting information from any device of this type. This of course assumes the hurdle of gaining access to the device has been overcome.

Finally, when the phenomenon of Bring Your Own Device (BYOD) is added to that scenario, the stakes are raised enormously. It has become a major challenge to the forensics expert to effectively collect all necessary data, and an equally major challenge to management to protect the enterprise's information in such a potentially "leaky" digital environment.

Cell Phones and Tablets

In today's mobile-oriented computing and communications world, smart phones are more powerful than most personal computers were, barely ten years ago. Smart phones routinely come with storage of 16, 32, or 64 GB and so do most tablets, either by the use of on-board memory or added memory using secure digital (SD) cards or universal serial bus (USB) flash drive devices. With this level of storage, substantial information can be stored in the memory of the small mobile device in the employee's pocket.

The difference between these add-on memory devices and computers is that the memory is typically not easily removable from the portable device. So it is

CONTENTS

imperative to collect the content of that device's memory within a very short time after the triggering event has taken place.

Most cell phone and tablet operating systems (Android and Apple's iOS are the two most prominent in the market place) have built-in routines that reorganize or delete the data portion of the memory space to optimize device operations. One of the functions in these devices reorganizes or deletes data as soon as necessary to make free space available for the new data. The busier the device's user is, the more rapidly data is reorganized or deleted. This functionality creates the need for management to get possession of the device immediately, to make possible the prompt collection of any relevant data that might be on such a device.

Additionally, the process of data collection from mobile devices is not like the process of data collection from a traditional computer hard disk. The data on the mobile device is collected on a live real-time basis. That is, the ESI collection is made as the device runs, by sending commands to the operating system, instead of using a write blocker to isolate the evidence drive from the collection device, as in the traditional computer forensics. That is the reason forensic consultants mostly agree that mobile device forensics is not computer forensics in the traditional definition of the term.

What valuable information can be obtained through the process of collecting mobile device data besides the typical application information found in traditional computers? Retrievable information can include call logs, message logs, location information from GPS chips on-board, navigation data from map software, contacts, and other mobile-oriented applications, which are typically not active on traditional network computers.

In addition, there is cell phone software that can allow the user to communicate with other parties without recording the messages in traditional phone logs maintained by the carrier or the phone. In such cases, it is necessary to extract the messages from files located in the phone memory.

Laptops and Industrial Portable Devices

The development of portable computing has created a major shift in how computing is done as well as where it is done. This was brought about by the shrinking size of components, the exponential increase in the power of processors and the increase in battery life from hours to days. Most of today's laptop computers and computing tablets have more power on board and as much storage as office desktop systems.

Therefore, it is necessary to pay attention to the collection of these types of devices, whenever they are part of the landscape when the triggering event happens. In many industries (eg, chemical processing), the use of portable devices by employees is common. Those devices will contain information that could reveal critical data in the investigation of employee actions during implementation of a management directive or before, during and after a catastrophic event.

These laptops, tablet computers, and industrial computers can be processed in a manner similar to that needed for regular office computers, unlike their lightweight cousins the mobile tablets and smart phones.

BYOD—BRING YOUR OWN DEVICE ISSUES

The forensic field of mobile devices is complex enough, but complexity increased enormously when an enterprising group of managers devised the concept of BYOD as a way of saving money by not issuing company-owned mobile devices to the employees. Whether this development was purely coincidental to the development of designating groups of employees as "independent contractors" is completely beyond the scope of our discussion here. That is a management complexity which only tangentially can become a forensic complexity.

Since the BYOD trend began a few years ago it has taken a firm hold, with a large number of variants in the implementation and management of electronic device activities.

Many organizations have done a fine job in the process, implementing employee-owned device use via legal agreements, thoughtfully developed and well-enforced policies, and methods by which personal user information is segregated from company information, by the use of encrypted folders, separate memory areas, or other innovative techniques.

On the other hand, there are many organizations that have implemented this process simply to save money, and have neglected the legal and technical implications of properly handling this commingled information.

Let's assume for a moment that an employee is allowed or even told to use his personal iPhone for company use, at his expense. Let's further assume that no written agreement (signed by the employee) exists between him and the employer for the care and custody of the iPhone or of any of the data on it. What happens if the employee suddenly leaves under less than friendly circumstances? Is the company data essentially abandoned to him? Or is there a duty by the employee (meaning, enforceable by the employer) to erase the company data from his phone? Is the employee obligated to allow the former employer to examine and collect the content of the phone? Can he be compelled by a court order post-employment to turn his phone over to the company? Can the employer use technology to remotely access the ex-employee's phone?

Changing the focus to the current employee: What about the lost, stolen, or left-in-a-bar phone? What about the "free after three" phone upgrade? What about the…? You get it.

And, by the way, your employee is the actual person on the contract for the phone, right? As in, who is the actual legal owner entitled to control access?

In many states, these are unanswered legal questions. The answers will only come through time and expense spent in the courts. That is not much comfort to the ex- or exasperated employer.

If a company plans to implement BYOD, it needs to first develop a thoughtful and clearly expressed written policy, have it signed by each employee, then implement and enforce it fully, with the appropriate legal and data protections necessary to protect both the employee and the company in a fair and reasonable manner.

We note in passing that National Labor Relations Board/US Department of Labor regulations and enforcement actions may affect an employer's right to control an employee's use of privately-owned digital devices. This is particularly urgent in the context of email and social media. We urge you to confer with an experienced labor/employment law specialist before proceeding with any BYOD plans.

Naturally, when the triggering event happens, it will be management's job to explain the situation to the forensic consultant on the Team, including the possible necessity to hire someone else to find the involved employees and their wandering devices.

WITHOUT PREDICTING

Even as we write, more and "improved" personal devices and applications are arriving at desks across the world. We have no intention of trying to keep up with all of them. But you need to. The basic issues related to the device usefulness in the business context remain, subject to your thoughtful consideration of how new data locations should change your approach to non-system data collection.

CHAPTER 6

Collecting Data

UNDERSTANDING THE SYSTEMS IN THE ORGANIZATION: INFORMATION GOVERNANCE

The forensic consultant on the Team must understand the organization's systems. Otherwise the consultant will fail in his or her primary task: to advise the Team's litigation lawyers as they prepare to respond to the Rule 34 requirements: to allow for the inspection of electronic documents (ESI) at the location of storage, and to be able to arrange for copying of the ESI for further inspection away from the premises.

The complex set of practices dictated by the Rules has been filtered down to the terms "collection or acquisition." This is the forensic copying of digital data for legal examination and evaluation, and for possible future presentation as evidence in resolving a legal dispute.

A secondary reason for the forensic consultant to have a prior understanding of the information systems is to know more efficiently where to go when a legal dispute arises between parties. In organizations that have done this homework in advance, the costs of collecting the appropriate ESI are far lower than those that leave this task to the last minute after an incident occurs, or even later.

For example, organizations that have mapped their data properly can conduct forensic triage when the litigation hold is issued. These organizations only collect very targeted data from specific system locations pertinent to the elements of the case at hand, saving substantial costs in searching for and preserving the necessary ESI for analysis as evidence.

On the other hand, cases arise in which it is necessary to collect the ESI contents of a substantial number of computers in their entirety to assure that nothing is left to chance. In these cases, system data mapping before the triggering event is even more cost-effective, particularly if time is a significant issue in preservation.

WHY SYSTEM STRUCTURAL INFORMATION IS NECESSARY—THE DATA MAP

From the smallest to the largest company today, private or public, almost anywhere in the world, information systems play a vital role in the operation of the enterprise.

This also applies to most individuals in most of the countries around the world. Today, even in places like rural areas of Africa, cell phones are used as communication tools as well as banking terminals, to transact business among people. So even when a dispute has nothing to do directly with the electronics involved, there is a high probability that the device contains information that may change the interpretation of the facts.

For example, cell phones have been used to prove that an individual accused of a shooting, based on eyewitness testimony, was at a location other than the site of the incident in question. Another instance was a picture, along with cell transmission tower information, that placed the suspect at a location far away from the scene of an incident. A cell phone has proved the loss of competitive information that was transferred a few days before an employee's last workday at a firm.

The issue is not just collecting the evidence data, but also properly analyzing the background metadata created by the device or system itself about that evidence data. The metadata informs the forensic analysis, so the analyst can accurately answer the questions posed by the lawyers.

There is a need for the attorney and forensic examiner in the case to communicate with each other in a clear manner to effectively find the actual independent facts. The forensic examiner must understand the underlying factual questions in order to give the "whole truth" which supports appropriate legal arguments on behalf of the client.

There are attorneys who abandon any responsibility for finding the digital evidence by simply saying to the IT personnel or forensic consultant, "find some smoking guns." These attorneys are demonstrating their own digital incompetence by forcing the analyst to figure out what the important legal and evidence issues are.

This is a disservice to the forensic expert as well as to the client, since most forensic experts are not lawyers. These lawyers need to be honest with themselves and with the forensic expert if their ability with information systems is limited to pushing the "Start" button on their computers to check email. No one should let ego issues damage a client's case, when simply asking the forensic expert to exchange ideas about the factual and legal questions would save the situation.

Situations such as these, where the lawyer is unaware of the client's system structure, and therefore fails to communicate the critical factual as well as legal questions to the expert, lend themselves to forcing the forensic expert to cover all the system's bases, whether appropriate or not. The forensic expert is compelled to retrieve and analyze massive quantities of clearly irrelevant information, in order to prevent the possibility of being surprised later by the client, the attorney, or the opposing party, by failing to discover a critical piece of information (especially when that information contradicts the client's position).

Cases have arisen over the years where forensic experts have been sued for "malpractice" due to a lack of work being performed. Lawyers willing to learn even a little bit about the digital world could easily avoid these disasters by taking advantage of the forensic expert's willingness to talk about designing effective forensic strategies based on the structure from which data can be found.

We suggest that lawyers who are part of a Team are less likely to make the errors described above, because they will be in a situation where structural information about digital evidence location is most likely to be effectively exchanged.

THE PEOPLE WHO SHOULD KNOW

Depending on the size of an organization, there are a variety of people who know how and where ESI is stored. If the client is a small office, the owner is likely going to be one of the most knowledgeable IT persons. If it is a Fortune 500 company, there will be departments full of people with a high level of knowledge about how and where information is stored.

If I, a computer forensics consultant, could speak to my forensic clients as an attorney, I would tell my clients that a few hours to compile a list now of who knows what and where the data is located will be a worthwhile endeavor that will pay off in the future when the notice of the triggering event arrives. The client saves time, confusion and misunderstanding at the worst possible moment. The lawyers and forensic experts save time and aggravation, which are direct sources of cost to the client.

Let us take as an example, a small company with one hundred employees, a two-person IT department, and a five-person accounting department. The remaining employees are all either in sales or operations. In such a situation, the IT department's knowledge is going to be limited, probably not going beyond what the installed systems and applications in use by the business are. Their role is simply to support the activities of the company and maintain the servers and workstations in working condition.

In such cases it is advantageous for a company to establish a relationship with a forensic consultant before any triggering event or litigation is in progress. The consultant would efficiently create and then assist the company to maintain records about the computer systems, mapping the locations of various kinds of data for the future date when an incident occurs. When an incident does occur, this same consultant is ready to go back into action, to work with the attorneys and client to narrow the amount of information to be collected as appropriate to the circumstances.

I can't count how many times a forensic consultant is asked to jump into a situation where there is no knowledge of the location of any of the data, or how the system is interacting with it. Meanwhile the attorneys expect a magical response to the digital evidence issues in the case. This results in a higher-than-necessary expenditure of expert hours, both legal and forensic, learning the particulars of the operating system.

This excess expenditure could easily have been avoided if system mapping had been done much earlier. The task could have been achieved in the course of normal operations by assigning tasks to various people on the job (accountants and IT) who work with the computer system every day.

Also, such data mapping records could easily have been kept updated as a routine procedure, eliminating any questions about the accuracy of the records when the critical moment arrives.

Generally, the organizational positions (not all-inclusive) that have working knowledge of the location and management of data (without regard for the size of the enterprise) are:

    Accountants/bookkeeping
    Computer technicians
    IT managers
    IT directors
    Database administrators
    Programmers
    Network technicians
    IT security
    Chief information officer (CIO)
    Chief information security officer (CISO)
    Data owners
    Data managers
    Principals and owners
    Service providers (outside backups)
    Internet service providers
    Wireless carriers

It is obviously useful to have HR's input on analogous job titles, particularly in organizations that have undergone mergers, where different titles may be retained that may not accurately reflect the current work allocations related to the computer systems and related devices.

IDENTIFYING THE FORENSIC CONSULTANT AND INTERNAL FORENSIC TEAM

What makes a forensic consultant valuable to your legal effort? It is that most forensic consultants have had extensive training and experience in information systems. They generally come from the discipline of computer operations, and are responsible for the day-to-day running of systems. Or they come to forensic consulting from the information security field. In addition, at some point in their careers they have received training in digital forensics, and have learned the intricate protocols necessary to accurately preserve and examine the digital information collected in support of dispute resolution.

So, how do you select a qualified forensic consultant? In the early days, the 1990s, it was based on reputation and referrals. Today, the forensics profession has advanced to the level of certifications and education programs. There are a number of certifications. Some have more requirements than others, such as those that represent the holder as a qualified individual in the field.

For example, the Digital Forensics Certification Board (DFCP) and the Certified Cyber Forensics Professional (CCFP) from the International Information System Security Certification Consortium, Inc. (ISC²) have very substantial requirements in the areas of knowledge, experience and ethics. We have listed the websites for both these organizations in the Resources Appendix at the back of this book.

As the industry continues to mature, the process of vetting individuals in the forensic consulting field will continue to mature, under the purview of independent certification organizations that review the individual's background, experience and education, and test the knowledge of the candidate prior to issuing a certificate. In addition, these organizations monitor the continuing education of the certificated individuals, along with their conformance to ethics and professional rules.

Many mega-size organizations like Wal-Mart, the Department of Defense, Chase Bank, and other large entities have invested resources in developing internal forensic teams. The internal forensic team handles the digital preservation and analysis process within the enterprise. These team members are trained as well as or better than any forensic consultant on the outside. In these enterprises, the corporate legal counsel's office will receive the results of an internal investigation. The report outlines the available factual information plus the means, ways, and sources of information supporting the entity's legal strategy for their case.

But this represents at most a couple of hundred organizations on a worldwide scale, leaving the rest of the enterprises in the world and their attorneys to select a competent outside digital forensic consultant who can deliver sound results.

DATA COLLECTION STRATEGIES, LOOKING FORWARD

I have yet to find an organization that can honestly claim that it has never been in litigation and will never be in litigation in the future. Planning and information gathering will expedite confirmation of where the information is located, what the appropriate information is, and how much to collect (triage) in relation to the situation. This process has been called proportionality by some parties, providing enough to prove the point of the case without spending more in the effort than necessary.

An organization that knows its data locations, systems, and processing methods, and the ways to analyze specific preserved data's relationship to the legal dispute, can effectively deliver reliable digital evidence in a short amount of time with highly focused results. This can be a strategic advantage in pretrial settlement negotiations, and in narrowing the scope of a case quickly.

On the other hand, if everyone in your organization is stumbling around, getting in each other's way, trying to figure out what information there is and where it is, and whether it still exists, then you will have to pay the price in money and lost productivity for results that over-produce information, or that produce surprises by allowing the other side to find smoking guns and benefit from the chaos in your overall process.

Clearly your entire organization benefits if you have done your data-collection planning in advance by system data mapping under the guidance of a knowledgeable forensic consultant, and have already installed appropriate data search software as recommended, for use on an instant's notice. Your Team will be ready, and your organization can get on with doing business.

CHAPTER 7

Teamwork Prep for Data Management

GATHERING SYSTEMS OPERATING INFORMATION FOR DIGITAL FORENSIC USE

In order to have a good understanding of your organization's overall data use, you as a Team have to gather and maintain specific knowledge. On the big-picture side you need to gather the data location, data control, and manner in which data of various types is used.

Ignorance creates confusion. When organizations fail to accomplish this information-gathering task in advance, for whatever reason, any incident becomes a major disruption, a fire drill of collecting everything there is, just in case, relevant to the dispute or not, so as not to miss a critical piece of information. The regular data management routines are disrupted, useless information is retained, systems may become inaccessible at critical moments and regular business operations are put on a chaotic basis, pending the "all clear" when the IT mob has left the operations area in disarray and retreated to do whatever IT people do. No organization needs this.

It takes a disciplined organization to maintain up-to-date records of its systems and data storage. At times it may be nearly impossible, especially when there have been major system upgrades, merged or acquired systems in corporate takeovers, and/or so-called legacy systems, where digital information is maintained on more than one system. These are critical moments for institutional memory of the prior system operations to be gathered quickly and preserved with great care.

This overall system-data information effort is called configuration management. It requires that every time there is a change to any part of the computer system or the manner in which data is stored, it is logged with precision into the configuration records. The configuration records assist the IT personnel in knowing the location of data along with the type of data at that location.

In-House Counsel's Perspective

Most in-house attorneys are on the front lines of incident response and ESI preservation, unless their department has specifically delegated this function to outside counsel or another department such as the information security department. If you are in the position of in-house counsel, then your primary goals are to alert the proper in-house and outside Team members immediately upon the occurrence of a triggering event, then to limit the scope of data collected and the production of materials in pretrial discovery to those items necessary to support the client's case.

In-house counsel needs to develop and maintain a communication line to the IT department prior to occurrence of any incidents in order to understand the limitations and obstacles to collecting data needed to resolve specific types of events. This is an appropriate element in the establishment and initial training of your incident-response Team.

For example, in a sexual harassment case, if you as counsel know who the key players are, and where the data elements are located for each of them, then you only need to direct collection and preservation of those items by the IT members of the Team. You can then conduct your preliminary investigation of the allegations to advise management of the presence or absence of any evidence of harassment directed to the alleged victim. In this case as an example, the examiner would collect email, social media, and other application data used to communicate among the key players, as well as the usual non-ESI evidence, such as employee statements.

The Litigator's Perspective

The outside counsel or litigation counsel has the burden of representing the client to opposing counsel and the court. The litigator is charged by Rule 26(f)(3) with having sufficient knowledge about the client's computer systems to negotiate with the opposing counsel on the amount of data and the manner in which the data will be produced in pretrial discovery. This is obviously not a "legal" skill.

In order to achieve the goals of minimizing and managing the collection of evidence effectively, which includes a working knowledge of its location, litigators need to have someone who guides them in learning the basics of computer architecture. That way, the litigators will understand, at least in concept, the location of the various types of ESI and the manner in which it can be produced, along with the advice as to the most efficient manner to produce the evidence.

It is appropriate for the organization's regular litigation attorneys to train with the Team at an early stage, when the ESI location and data mapping are considered. That way they will be able to consider ESI discovery strategies at leisure rather than in a panic on the way to the Rule 26(f) "meet and confer." More about that later.

The Forensic Consultant's Perspective

The role of the forensic consultant is to serve as a facilitator in helping the in-house and litigation attorneys understand how to achieve best compliance with the Rules, court requirements, and the goals of the case in using digital evidence. This of course can only be achieved if the attorneys take the necessary step of engaging the services of the consultant.

There are many cases where this important step is ignored until very late in pretrial discovery. Because of such late engagement, the collection and forensic analysis of evidence becomes more costly and difficult, if not completely ineffective, particularly if the litigators have made unwise or even ignorant choices in the initial Rule 26(f) evidence production negotiations.

In most cases, it is advantageous to engage the forensic consultant early to assist in training the Team. Even in an on-call capacity, the consultant can be ready to join the Team at the time of a triggering event. This gives the Team the advantage in structural planning for identification and collection of digital evidence.

In addition, if there are technical issues with implementing the litigation hold to preserve ESI, the forensic consultant can develop strategies and workarounds ahead of time for the process to take place effectively.

Most forensic consultants' interest is that the client presents evidence in a manner that reflects an organized approach to locating, preserving, and analyzing digital evidence, and that such an approach accounts for the evidence presented by clear and forensically-appropriate documentation. That way, questions about the collection and preservation processes are minimized, and the reliability of the evidence is clear.

It is surprising to see that in many instances improperly-trained "consultants" will present digital evidence without adequate support, origin documentation and/or supporting documents. I am also amazed at how often digital evidence is destroyed, for example by converting the original electronic files into TIFF images, which converts searchable files with metadata into nonsearchable photograph-style images.

Of course, if the goal of the opponent's ESI production strategy is to slow down discovery by taking advantage of the Team's assumed digital ignorance, then allowing them to indulge in such strategies in digital evidence production will have the desired effect of impeding progress in the case. A competent forensic consultant will immediately recognize these efforts for what they are, and alert the Team through litigation counsel. When the tactic is recognized, a legal counterattack can be mounted with the consultant's assistance, to force proper handling of digital evidence, to assure that the opponent is accurately accounting for the data in their client's systems, and to shine some bright light on the aggressive litigators and incompetent consultants who participate in evidence manipulation.

The IT Department's Perspective

The information technology department is the operational custodian for all the organization's electronic information. IT is also the focal point for coordinating the collection of digital information in case of a legal dispute or crime. The IT department operates the equipment where the data resides. IT personnel know the usage, reliability, and processing payload of their equipment. They speak its language and know it intimately.

All IT department personnel need to be kept in the Team's information loop from the beginning for several reasons. Among them, they know the structural information the Team will need. They need to be able to aggregate their knowledge of where things are within the system(s), for their Team representative to bring to the rest of the Team.

IT also operates as a sub-unit of the Team when the triggering event occurs. Every member of the IT department must be suitably trained to react to the litigation hold alert in ways appropriate to their skills. Any time there is a litigation hold notice issued, the IT representative on the Team needs to send the alert to everyone in the IT department, so one IT person does not inadvertently undo the work of another, and so every necessary non-routine step gets done. In terms of the structure of the system, this is completely in IT's hands.

When they are informed by the Team to at least temporarily stop the deletion of data from the systems relevant to the issues identified in the hold notice, they will make their own decisions, in consultation with the forensic consultant, about how to act effectively. This is why it is critical that in-house counsel's Team member inform the IT department's Team member anytime there is an event that requires a litigation hold. This will allow IT to stop data pruning, prevent file deletions of emails and other high volume systems, and preserve back-up tapes as necessary.

It is the responsibility of the IT department to manage and document the configuration of the systems under their direct control. It is also IT's responsibility to understand the controls and management configuration of systems outsourced to third parties by the company. The recent trend to outsourcing of information systems to hosting and cloud vendors has led management teams to believe that they have been absolved of any responsibility for the information residing in those outsourced systems. This is far from legal reality, and can lead to surprises and other serious problems, when the data residing with the third party vendors cannot be retrieved or cannot be fully retrieved to preserve digital evidence.

DATA INVENTORIES MANAGEMENT: WHAT DATA AND WHY

The concept of the data inventory has evolved from the security classification system for data in government files, such as classified military and related defense records. But the concept is applicable across many other industries in the current age of proliferating electronic information.

This concept of knowing what data is being stored and the reason for such storage can help inform the process of data collection by knowing the systems and locations of types of data likely to be relevant to a dispute.

The data inventory concept is also applicable to the development and maintenance of an effective security posture, by allowing the allocation of security resources to the data elements that are most sensitive to the organization (eg, the "secret formula" or drawings for a new product). Company management should consider the implementation of a data inventory that is updated on a regular basis to support their security and legal response obligations.

The point of a data inventory is not to produce yet more data, but to analyze the movement of data across all of the organization's systems and devices. This will identify, among the many inconsistent data names and definitions, the data that are of ongoing or current use to the organization. Outdated information of purely historical interest and data that simply was never deleted are also identified by this process, which is useful for "housekeeping" purposes by IT as well as management.

The data inventory output must be structured with ongoing usefulness in mind. The identification of data moving within your systems and devices allows the data inventory analyst to categorize data as useful, duplicate, inconsistent, or historical versions, as well as data that are being preserved for various corporate planning purposes. This output then allows the analyst to prepare a data dictionary that will effectively allow identification of key corporate data and associated data structures for later data retrieval in the event of a security challenge or a litigation hold.

Please note that we did not say this process was going to be easy. We just said that in our experience it is going to be necessary.

What is a Data Inventory and What Should it Contain?

Inventorying the data that moves between system locations accomplishes two things: it identifies the most valuable data elements in use, and it also helps to identify data that is not high-value, as it is not being shared or used. This approach also provides a way to tackle initial data quality efforts by identifying the most "active" data used by the business. It ultimately helps the data management team in IT understand where to focus its efforts and how to prioritize accordingly.

Typically, a data inventory will contain the type of data and the system hosting it, along with its value to the organization. For example, in many organizations information is collected simply for historical reasons, or because we have done it this way all along. Instead, it is a good idea to review the type of information being collected from customers, vendors, and other third parties, to see if the data is still of any value to the organization.

Also, this process can serve to identify information that may be sensitive due to its personally identifiable nature (eg, social security numbers, driver's license numbers, etc.). This data identification is critical for many reasons, some of which we have discussed in the evidence-preservation context. We emphasize this particular data because federal regulations highly restrict disclosing it, but many litigators and information managers do not think of it in the context of evidence preservation and discovery.

The data inventory should include the type of data and the system or systems that host it. An obvious example is email information. Most people would think that an email server would be the location in which emails are stored. But instead, what most readers are not aware of is that applications like Microsoft Outlook allow for the creation of local PST files databases, which can store emails also. This scenario would allow the user to move emails from his server folders to a local email database that would be stored on his assigned personal computer. If this is not accounted for, it would be easy to miss locally stored emails in the key players' and other custodian workstations and their various devices.

If this type of storage diversion is not desired, then the IT department needs to configure user workstations, so as not to allow for the creation of PST files locally. If it is desired or at least acceptable, the data inventory should note this special condition in email storage, so as not to mislead the Team in the litigation hold process.

Managing and Updating Data Inventories

A data inventory, once completed, should be maintained on a regular basis to keep its value. It should be visited at least once a year, but more often if major system changes are implemented between annual reviews. It is necessary to look at the data inventory as a living document that is updated with as much frequency as is necessary to keep its value to the user.

In addition, if the organization has major personnel changes, such as corporate restructuring of divisions or departments, merger with another entity, etc., the data inventory needs to be revisited to accommodate new organizational lines of authority and other structural issues. In such circumstances maintaining the old data inventory for a reasonable time during the transition, along with the new data inventory, may be useful. When the corporate adjustment is ended, the "historical" version needs to be sent off to the non-operations archives.

It is important to keep in mind that the point of this is to have a living document that must be adjusted and updated regularly, so that it is accurate at the unexpected moment when finding specific data becomes necessary.

DATA DESTRUCTION POLICIES AND HOLD MANAGEMENT: WHO DECIDES AND WHO ACTS

Data destruction policies are normally implemented in IT environments because of the large amount of data that is collected in most information systems. For example, in most mid-size business email systems, the average email user receives over 100 emails per day, every day of the year, or over 39,000 emails per year per employee. If a company stores every one of these, it will soon need a substantial amount of storage just for email. Therefore, most companies prune or delete from their systems on a regular basis all emails designated by the recipients as "deleted."

But when a triggering event indicates that litigation is likely in the foreseeable future, it is necessary to at least temporarily suspend the email deletion routine until a backup of the email server is made, to ensure that a critical piece of communication is not lost.

The issue of routine data destruction policies and practices, and the prompt, effective suspension of those policies and practices, is one that can easily be the subject of early training for the Team. The exact extent of the routine destruction policies and the specific steps in the destruction practices are known to one or more persons somewhere in the organization. The Team needs that information, through its various members.

The in-house counsel Team member is responsible for promptly informing the IT Team member that an event has triggered a litigation hold in the organization. The IT members of the Team must work with the Team's legal members, as soon as the triggering event is identified to IT by legal, to stop the routine data destruction procedure immediately.

This is an area in which your organization needs a clear procedure for the legal department to alert the Team (including management and IT) of a triggering event. This alert will implement the litigation hold notice drafting by identifying all the key players, and will notify all the affected personnel through issuing the written litigation hold notice.

The training in data destruction policies and procedures will pay off in getting the Team into action as quickly as possible after the triggering event. This quick response is beneficial from the data destruction perspective, by collecting and preserving the relevant information from running systems, rather than from archival sources that are usually slower and require more cost and effort to collect from.

Managing the Hold When Data Destruction is Suspended—Choking on Data

When the routine data destruction process is turned off, you have a serious problem. How do you mitigate the "choking on data" syndrome?

In many systems, once a litigation hold is implemented and routine data destruction is suspended, the systems can only hold so much additional information before operational issues develop, like running out of storage for continuing operations of the enterprise.

A plan of action needs to be prepared ahead of time to prevent this from occurring. In today's world, portable media storage (hard drives) is inexpensive. Readily-available devices hold ever-larger amounts of data. The best practice is to move the collected information to media that is dedicated to the dispute—media that have already been purchased and stored in IT's work area for this occasion. An example of this is that in 2015, a 4 TB (terabyte) hard disk can be purchased for as little as $140.

This allows for the storage of case evidence in a small amount of space, and allows for the preservation of that evidence for the life of the case, while freeing up the organization's systems to return to normal operations. When we have worked with clients with large amounts of data to be analyzed to identify the actual evidence, we move the collected data to portable disk arrays that not only maintain data integrity by using RAID5 technology, but are also extremely portable. Thus, we are able to maintain the data while transferring the files to the appropriate forensic laboratory for further analysis, with minimal disruption to day-to-day operations.

HOW LONG DO WE HOLD THIS DATA?

Generally, case evidence is held by the parties until the case and all possible appeals are completed, so that the case (or portions of it) can be retried, if required by the courts. This is the standard practice in evidence storage in the US federal and state court systems.

It is possible to reduce the amount of data stored long-term (including post-trial). During the initial negotiation process, and as the discovery process develops, the legal members of the Team can obtain agreements (called stipulations) from the other side about the scope of the actual disputed facts. Those stipulations will reduce the data that will be needed to resolve the dispute. This would include agreements to dispose of information you have saved under the "hold" but which will not be relevant to any of the legal issues identified in the case pleadings, at trial, or on appeal. Careful coordination between the Team's legal, IT, and forensic consultant members will ensure that you can safely dispose of the unnecessary data gathered under the litigation hold while continuing to preserve the remaining relevant data.

REGULATORY REQUIREMENTS AND INDUSTRY NORMS ON DATA DESTRUCTION

In many industries, due to either regulatory requirements or industry norms, the deletion of data from information systems is either accelerated or not implemented for certain classes of data.

It is important that the forensic consultant, legal counsel, regulatory compliance supervisor, and management members of the Team understand the exact extent of these practices and how they affect the organization's data management. With that regulatory and industry information, litigation holds can be promptly and properly implemented in accordance with these norms. In addition, the response will already be in place for any later criticism regarding the scope of the litigation hold.

Understanding these industry practices and regulatory requirements is a crucial component of understanding the limits and constraints in the litigation hold process for your organization. It needs to be part of your Team's formation and early training, so all Team members know these special restrictions on data handling. In addition, new members rotating onto the Team can easily get up to speed on such issues.

PERSONALLY IDENTIFIABLE INFORMATION (PII) RESTRICTIONS

"Personally identifiable information" (PII) includes, for example, birth dates, names of under-age individuals, addresses, passport numbers, health care information, social security/medicare numbers, driver's license numbers, bank account numbers, and similar personal information. As a quick rule of thumb, if you think it probably has value to identity thieves, it should be treated as PII.

If information relevant to the case contains PII as defined by federal law and regulations, or other personal information, these particular elements of the information must be protected from disclosure. Unless required by a specific court order, all PII must be taken out of the ESI before it is produced to opposing parties.

All federal trial courts have standing orders that require PII to be blocked in all documents filed with the court because the information in those documents becomes a public record. The courts also restrict use of documents as evidence offered in court unless all PII has been redacted (covered up) or otherwise blocked.

We note in passing that some software programs that purport to redact or otherwise conceal PII in electronic documents are ineffective, for the simple reason that the person viewing the document can use many common word-processing programs to cancel the blocking instruction. Be warned.

Even worse, in this author's experience in forensic examination of digital evidence, I have from time to time received ESI containing medical records, social security numbers, drivers' licenses, and other personal information from the opposing party's business records, when that content was not requested nor required to resolve the case. It was clear to me that the personal information was produced due to improper processing techniques by less than competent forensic consultants and/or IT personnel ignorant about that requirement.

It is important that the work of forensic consultants be reviewed by the attorneys before producing it to the opposing party, on a sampling basis at a minimum, to be sure that industry and regulatory guidelines and federal law are not violated in the production of ESI.

DATA, READY FOR THE TEAM

Your Team will not be effective if it is formed and trained in a state of information chaos. The initial Team members need to be your forensic consultant and IT representatives. With management's cooperation and encouragement, this group will prepare the groundwork for your larger Team to train and work effectively.

CHAPTER 8

Data Policies and Procedures—Get the Details

In this chapter we are going to guide the entire Team through the types of institutional information that need to be understood in detail by all individuals involved in data collection before the process begins. This ensures that proper strategies are executed to capture the real-world data, rather than just the theoretical data reflected in general policy statements. Only through the combined knowledge of the entire Team will the litigation hold be effective in capturing the real evidence to resolve the dispute.

UNDERSTANDING SPECIFIC INFORMATION FOR THE ESI PRESERVATION PROCESS

The individuals who will direct the forensic collection of ESI after a litigation hold is issued must have at hand the complete details of the organization's policies and procedures for managing and storing its electronic information for day-to-day operational purposes.

Examples of these policies and procedures include data backup policy details for the system: how often, how long, when tapes are re-used, how they are stored for use in the cycle, whether there are separate schedules for different sectors of the system, etc.

If these details are not understood, mistakes and improper assumptions are likely to be made. These mistakes may result in evidence being irretrievably lost, a situation that in some cases could be catastrophic to the success of the case. (Remember the *Zubulake* and *Pension Committee* cases we discussed in Chapter 2.)

In-House Counsel's Perspective

Corporate counsel needs to understand how the IT department handles the information entrusted to it. This is a critical step in the process of being able to draft a hold notice that IT can actually use for effective ESI collection in support of outside counsel in litigation. Obviously it is also critical in obtaining

CONTENTS

the on-the-ground facts needed to properly advise management. If this preliminary educational step is not taken, then the lawyers essentially abdicate control over the collection process and all that follows in the litigation process after ineffective data preservation.

This ignorance on the part of the people who hire them is why you see vendors that literally charge thousands of dollars for collections that are overbroad and in many cases out of control. The primary driver for this is that most vendors charge by the Gigabyte (GB) of storage collected, so the more storage collected the higher the charges are for the process. In the absence of specific instructions, this author has seen vendors collect the content of all the servers and workstations within the entire business and, in addition, collect and process all backup tapes also in the possession of the client. This has led to cases where the fees for processing the digital evidence have exceeded the amount in dispute.

An example is the following case analysis, from the Exterro, Inc. blog on ESI cases and news by Mike Hamilton, J.D., Senior Manager, E-Discovery Programs:

> In *Connecticut General Life Insurance*, a discovery dispute arose around the defendant's supplemental responses to the plaintiff's, Connecticut General Life Insurance, additional production requests of 219 GB of emails. The defendant objected to the plaintiff's requests for production because the cost of the production, when considered against the amount in controversy within the case, rendered production "unduly burdensome." The defendant produced documentation to the court showing cost breakdowns for searching and producing the requested ESI, along with other cost estimates for alternative search parameters based on the plaintiff's discovery requests.
> To fully produce 219 GB of emails from 19 different email accounts, the defendant provided documentation that it would cost over $121,000 to index, filter and process the information, exceeding the amount at stake in the case (Note: This cost estimate did not include project management or attorney review costs.)
> Based on the documentation and metrics produced by the defendant, the court ruled for the defendant, stating, "The Court will not order Defendant to absorb the incredible expense associated with responding to these five RFPs (requests for production), especially when Defendant has been working to produce documents and information in response to Plaintiff's various other discovery requests." The court found the e-discovery cost projections as "persuasive, credible, and reliable," which proved that the cost of producing the requested emails, "far exceeds what is at stake in the instant litigation, and therefore, the Court concludes the requests are unduly burdensome." Even though the court noted that the plaintiff requests may be helpful, the fact that the plaintiff will and already had received a significant amount of ESI from the defendants, combined with

the high costs of producing the plaintiff's additional ESI heavily favored the court siding with the defendant. The court did leave the plaintiff the option to fund the costs for additional e-discovery themselves.

The Litigator's Perspective

From the litigation attorney's view, the collection of information that may be evidence focuses on proving the client's arguments in court. In many instances attorneys fail to understand, and therefore fail to effectively use, the information about digital evidence developed by the forensics expert.

For example, in a civil suit accusing your client of hacking another company's computer system, you need evidence to prove the client did not hack the victim's computer. Your digital expert will need to examine many sectors of the opponent's computer system, as well as the computer system your client allegedly used in the hack, to prove that the information the opponent is offering as evidence is speculative and does not support the inferences made from it by the other side. Without guidance in examining the systems, the expert will either have to massively over-analyze or engage in unfounded speculation of his own about data movements in the two computer systems. If your expert has reliable information about how data is created, moved, and stored, the speculative element goes away (along, hopefully, with the lawsuit against your client).

Regardless of the side on which you sit as counsel, the road to success begins with your functional understanding of the sources of information within the computer system. With that basic understanding, you are able to make use of the information brought to you by the Team and developed by you through your forensic expert witness's analysis. You not only can have confidence in your own evidence, you are ready to use your opponent's lack of knowledge to your advantage. Based on this author's personal experience, a well-analyzed and researched computer forensic analysis of your data, showing you are ready to rely on properly preserved ESI from all reasonably possible sources within the system, will get a dismissal or a settlement in a significant percentage of cases.

This is due to the fact that no one wants to spend money to lose an argument. It is very difficult to successfully mischaracterize a well-documented universe of digital evidence. If it's all there, and you can prove that, you hold the upper hand in the argument over "the whole truth, and nothing but." Now you can concentrate on the legal issues on which you have some leverage, including the doubtful completeness of the opponent's digital evidence.

The Forensic Consultant's Perspective

Most forensic consultants fall into two categories: those who are part of a larger organization and must follow their company's program, and those who are independent and can generally develop strategies as the case demands. It is important for the consultant to be sure the hiring attorneys understand these differences.

It is also important for the consultant to understand the precise scope of the job. Does the lawyer already know in general the client's data policies and procedures? Does the lawyer know what specific assistance is needed from you in digital evidence collection, preservation, and analysis? Does the lawyer just want you to "find some good stuff" (whatever the lawyer thinks that might be)? Does the lawyer have some ESI to show you, and just want you to agree that it is what he wants it to be?

These issues are important since it can be dangerous for any lawyer to simply take everything the client provides at face value. Consider the case of tech company *LBDS Holding Co. v ISOL Technology*, which lit up the legal blogosphere in the spring of 2014. Making a long, ugly story comparatively short, after winning a $24 million jury verdict based on violations of a contract and theft of trade secrets, the plaintiff's lead trial lawyer had to respond to accusations by the defendants that the winning "evidence" was in fact forged by his clients, the plaintiffs. When he asked his clients about the documents, they admitted that they had forged not just one document but all the winning evidence (including creating a fictitious domain name and creating phony email traffic to support the other forged evidence). The company leaders also told the lawyer that they had all lied in testifying about the contract. The lawyer told his clients if they didn't notify the court about their actions, he would have to. They refused. He filed a motion to withdraw as counsel, informing the court of the facts he had discovered post-trial.

This example outlines the issues of evidence tampering by the client in order to assure a win for their side. The forensic consultant does not have real access to the preserved data taken from the system by individuals properly trained to do it correctly (and ethically). As a result the forensic consultant must assume (at his own peril) that what he is shown is "real" when he makes his data analysis and gives his conclusions about the data.

There have been a regrettably large number of instances through the years where one side or the other in an argument will delete information or create information in the computer system in order to improve the odds of a positive outcome in a case. See Chapter 2 for a few of them, and how they fared.

This is where there are important differences in the types of forensic consultants who may be required to look at the data. As a forensics expert, you need to know enough about the client's data policies and procedures for you to satisfy yourself on this subject. You should not accept a job unless you know that you will be able to give honest and complete answers to the lawyer and client about their data analysis needs. This is true whether you will be an expert witness at trial or whether you will be the Team's guide in properly identifying and preserving data for the litigation hold, and/or for your later forensic analysis.

In case we have given you the impression that it is only the client you need to worry about, here's one more horror story from the legal blogosphere, from summer, 2015, in the Denver, Colorado state court case of *Premium Pet Health, LLC v All American Pet Proteins, LLC, Craig A. Broughton, John F. Landers, Gary "Ron" Dean, and Michael Yousif* (Case No. 2014CV31356). Individual defendant John Landers was a former employee of the plaintiff, who left to start a competing company, the corporate defendant. After leaving his job with the plaintiff, Landers hired Yousif, a computer consultant, to help him remove more than 8,000 emails from the Inbox on his computer (which he had used in his former job), consisting of communications to and from co-workers, customers, and suppliers. Landers and Yousif kept no record of the deleted emails. While the massive email clean-up was in progress, Landers' new company hired lawyer Randall Miller to assist the new company with "transition issues." Miller is the managing partner of the Denver branch of a major national law firm, Bryan Cave LLP. Predictably, Landers' old company sued the new company and its owners. At Landers' request, Miller and his law firm expanded the engagement to include the lawsuit. A few days after the lawsuit was filed, Miller's colleague Sarah Hartley spoke with Landers and the other executives of the new client. When she found out about the 8,000 deleted emails, she confirmed that only the Inbox had been emptied. She ordered the executives to delete all email from the old company (now the plaintiff) in other parts of the computer, including the Outbox, Sent Mail, archives, Drafts and Trash/Deleted Files. Landers and Yousif complied. She then confirmed to her supervising partner, Miller, that she had done so. Later she attempted to defend herself by saying she thought a litigation hold had been issued by her firm to the client, although she had not checked to see whether it had (as if that were any excuse for such instructions). No litigation hold was issued for more than two weeks. Randall, knowing of both the pre-litigation and post-litigation destruction, reviewed and presented to the court an affidavit by Landers swearing that Landers had not had in his possession any documents of any kind belonging to his former company as of the day he quit. The judge, Chief Judge Michael Martinez, awarded the plaintiff an "adverse inference" instruction to the jury, so they could assume that whatever was destroyed was evidence in favor of the plaintiff and against the defendants. Judge Martinez also awarded attorneys' fees to be paid to the plaintiffs, for the cost of both the pre-litigation and post-litigation spoliation motions. The attorneys' fees were ordered against the corporate defendant, Landers, Yousif, and attorneys Sarah Hartley and Randall Miller, and their law firm.

While this is a serious matter for the lawyers who destroyed their careers, it is even more of a head's up warning to forensic consultants. If you see something in your forensic procedure that is even a little at odds with the facts you have been given by the lawyer and client, raise the red flag immediately. If you don't get an absolutely clear explanation, do not do what Mr. Yousif did and trash your own career.

The less these people want you to be part of the Team, and the less they want you to know about the company's data policies and procedures, the less you want to be associated with them. The concern about clients or lawyers who want to buy a specific answer from you should be of great importance to anyone in the digital consulting field.

SMALL, LARGE, FORTUNE 500 AND INTERNATIONAL— THE ECONOMICS OF STRUCTURE AND SCALE

The size of the organization makes a significant difference in the application of the recommendations in this book. Not everyone can fund and staff a complete in-house digital forensics laboratory like Wal-Mart does. Such a facility is not cost-effective and cannot be adequately supported by a smaller-sized company's budget. Let us help you look for ways to focus on the basics, plus additions that will increase effectiveness, while still respecting your budget.

In small organizations, as well as larger organizations with small IT departments, and highly decentralized enterprises, your cost-effective option is to develop a relationship with a properly-credentialed local, regional or national forensic consulting firm, depending on your budget. When an incident occurs, the consulting firm will already know the limits of your company's IT department and your computer system's data structure. At that time, your consultant will already know how to conduct the collection process, with minimal disruption and at the lowest cost possible. In a scenario of this type the cost per unit of data collected will be higher than what our Fortune 500 example pays for their collections. Nevertheless it will be more effective than to pick someone out the phone book after the incident and say, "We have a case and we need evidence collected immediately."

There are many medium-to-large law firms throughout the United States that recommend digital consultants from a list of approved vendors vetted by the firm's litigation support services department. However, you should be cautious in accepting such recommendations without additional inquiry about professional affiliations, certifications, etc. The consultant may be recommended for reasons other than competence or capabilities. This writer has taken over cases from recommended consultants where the consultants have missed critical evidence, improperly interpreted the results of their analysis, and did not conduct sufficient collections or analysis work to support their reports' conclusions. They had great marketing skills. They just didn't have great forensic skills.

For somewhat larger organizations, the IT staff can be trained to do collections, and to properly document their procedures, under the supervision of a consultant. This option is appropriate where there are sufficient IT employees to cover most company locations, and the IT employees at remote sites are trained on how to document the collection of evidence and forward it to the corporate office whenever necessary.

This outcome can also be achieved by the use of forensic data collection software systems recommended by the consultant. Such software can be deployed in the field at strategic locations, and remotely operated from a central location as and when needed.

Summarizing, it is important to develop a business relationship with a forensic consulting firm as part of your Team unless you have an internal depth of highly skilled capability that can be relied upon. Otherwise, it is far more cost effective to have the consultant you will use already in touch with the Team, prepared to deal with your systems and familiar with your IT operations in advance of the triggering event and litigation hold.

DELEGATION OF AUTHORITY FOR DATA DESTRUCTION POLICIES

Most businesses have some form of routine data destruction policy, to control the growth of stored information. Hopefully, that policy is generated by management, in writing, and actually enforced by the individuals who are charged with that task.

It is important for both the consultant and attorneys on the Team to understand which individuals in the organization are actually responsible for the control and suspension of these policies. The Team doesn't need the policy maker, it needs the policy enforcer on the Team.

Such staffing knowledge is critical for the Team, particularly when multiple litigation cases (from triggering event to trial) are ongoing simultaneously. In many cases litigation hold notices are issued to the managers and department heads who are directly involved with the key players in a case. But much too often, the litigation hold notice is not distributed to the data destruction policy enforcer and the data custodian/owners within the system. Therefore real-time data destruction operations continue without much regard for the unknown litigation hold.

It is critical that any individual identified as a key player or other data custodian be alerted to the existence and scope of the hold. Each of those individuals also needs to already understand the need to actively prevent deletion or mishandling of ESI evidence in a case. This danger of inadvertent ESI tampering or destruction by ignorant data custodians can be mitigated by conducting the collection of data as quickly as reasonably feasible.

For example, in a harassment case there are usually few individuals directly involved. It would make sense that as soon as a complaint is filed with the HR department (or otherwise comes to management's attention), the suspect's and complainant's computers, the system, and other electronic devices be collected and forensically imaged using appropriate protocols. That way no one can delete or modify data from the computers or devices. Management can make a preliminary evaluation of the complaint for further more leisurely action without danger of harm to the potential case. This will preserve evidence as well as bring to light any attempt by the accuser or an ill-intentioned third party to sabotage the accused employee.

In other data-driven cases, where the actual data-destruction control individuals are in the notice loop, a copy of a database done within a few days of an incident will save the need for a costly database recovery or restore in the future.

COMMUNICATING WITH THE RANK-AND-FILE EMPLOYEES

In almost every organization, employees work with two sets of data files: the files that are maintained by the organization for official records, and the files that each employee creates and maintains in order to achieve his job goals.

In many cases the contents of these two repositories of evidence are not the same when examined out of context, and may contain conflicting or confusing pieces of information. This can cause the forensic consultant and lawyers to view data as contradictory, instead of merely from different sources kept for different purposes.

It is important for the Team's lawyer members to clearly communicate to front-line employees who are actually producing and modifying data when a litigation hold goes into effect. In such cases, it will take more than simply sending a vague email or paper notice to the key players and other data custodians involved in the case.

For example, when the likely litigation will be complex rather than simple and straightforward, the hold notice must necessarily be complex. The Team must have a way to understand the types of information being generated by each actual data custodian, and where that data is, whether in the computer system, on individual workstations, or on other devices, in order to make accurate decisions for data preservation. Only in this way can the Team effectively alert the front-line employees who control the data in real time.

Let us for a moment assume a product: a complex pump and pipe design. The engineer in charge of the design runs a set of complex equations to determine the maximum limits of his design. In this case, every time the calculations are run, he saves the results along with spreadsheets on his computer, He also saves the "final" design to the project document repository. We have seen ESI evidence productions where the only document produced is the "final" calculation set, and the interim calculations are never collected from the engineer's personal workstation, where they are still located. Imagine the results of the engineer's oral deposition before trial (or worse, at trial) when the lawyer asks: "Was this the only calculation you ran in order to determine the maximum tolerances of the system?" and the engineer proceeds to answer "No, of course not." It will be a huge surprise for counsel to find this out at the last minute.

In some cases, clients have asked me to hold a meeting with identified data custodians, to explain what they need to do to comply with the litigation hold notice. In several cases, we found that employees had data repositories that the IT department did not even know existed. These IT people were never asked about data outside of the servers, or data destruction outside of the server's routine, so they never thought about destruction, preservation, and access in those other areas.

BUSINESS OPERATIONS (POLICY VERSUS REALITY)— WHO KNOWS WHAT AND WHO DOES WHAT?

Complete and accurate knowledge of the organization's internal operation is critical for effective data collection. After all, without a sure knowledge of all the structural facts, how can the lawyers and management evaluate litigation issues—to know when to defend and when to attack?

In such scenarios it is important for the Team to understand both the formal and informal operations of the organization as a whole. Why is this an important element? Because the informal organization may have information that is critical to the complete collection of ESI evidence.

This is especially critical in cases involving human resource issues, such as violation of company rules and policies, adverse terminations, etc. In these types of situations, it is important to understand those informal relationships and operations. These may point to the actual location of data showing the violation of policies and procedures. Such information prevents the surprise of an adverse witness or document surfacing at the most inappropriate time.

Sometimes the actual flow of information inside an organization does not follow the formal flowchart. Due to friendships, previous work relationships and other reasons, individuals will share information with those included in these informal connections. In many cases those communications can be the key to finding answers to why events took place and decisions were made.

In addition, staffing issues may reflect a different operating scenario than what is shown on the management chart. Shared support staff within a work group are often the source of "hidden" data, as for example when one secretary is completely absorbed in a major task, or away on vacation, so other support staff from the group (or even from outside the group) "fill in" as needed, leaving data on their workstations too. Again, this may be a situation that is news to HR, so on-the-ground inquiry by the Team is always appropriate.

Departments or Divisions That Operate Autonomously

Understanding the reality of the organization cannot be emphasized enough, as you have deduced. Missing key organizational components, or operations whose data is not centralized, can cause major problems or even irreversible losses in determining the universe of data sources in a collection effort.

Many national and international companies operate via holding companies with multiple autonomous divisions, which may or may not be separately incorporated, and may or may not be in different locations, so as to limit tax exposure and legal liability, and for other regulatory reasons. It is important to understand these intra-corporate and/or divisional relationships when forming, training and using the Team.

It is also important to know the actual level of operating autonomy of these units, while acknowledging any legal separation that may exist between entities, when issuing a litigation hold and collecting data. Without understanding these issues, the Team may inadvertently compromise corporate or regulatory separation, or relevant data may unintentionally be abandoned due to ignorance of ways to work through the corporate structure.

The management members of the Team should be thinking of divisional or corporate structural issues during your initial training, so these issues don't surface as a "gotcha" at an inopportune moment.

Divisions or Operations in Multiple States

Instituting an effective litigation hold in a multinational entity has challenges of its own, which we will discuss in detail in Chapter 12. The litigation hold is (at least comparatively) not as difficult when divisions and/or data centers are located in different states, since the litigation hold is itself a creation of the Federal Rules of Civil Procedure.

However, the Team must recognize in advance that different rules may apply from state to state, such as who can collect digital evidence and when. Merely for example, in Texas, any individual who collects digital information from a computer system or device for use in court must have a valid Private Investigator (Investigations Company) license issued by the State of Texas, or be a classified law enforcement officer, suitably certified for such digital collection of evidence. (Texas Occupations Code, section 1702.104(b).)

In other instances, states are developing unique laws and regulations for reporting to regulatory authorities and notifying credit card users, account holders, patients, etc., of data breaches. Some such breaches may also trigger federal reporting requirements. These may create different timelines for regulatory and law-enforcement reporting, collecting evidence for different purposes, and mitigating the incident, all of which directly affect the litigation hold and preservation protocols in those states.

DOCUMENT THE DAY-TO-DAY FLOW AND CONTROL OF ESI

The location and movement of data between units of the business (as well as within the portion of the computer system at each location) is important to know, so that the most effective point of collection can be determined for each type of data.

A good example is a complex industrial process where thousands of sensors are sending process information over a network to various databases. In such a case, it is important to understand the process in detail. There may be intermediate steps in the aggregation of the information along the way, such as a system controller that stores information for a period of time and then forwards the summarized data to a database server.

This is also applicable to mesh networks that collect data and transmit independent observations to a central location, that then must assemble the data components in order to make operational decisions with the information.

WHO HAS WHAT KINDS OF DEVICES, AND WHO KNOWS WHERE THEY ARE?

In today's computing universe, information is highly distributed. Despite the efforts of document-management professionals, not all information reaches the vaunted "central repository" of official documents. It is critical that the Team knows where each type of ESI is located, either temporarily or permanently.

We see many organizations with operating departments where IT skills are limited, and as a result these companies are contracting for outside IT services with little knowledge of what they need or what they are getting. A great price is of no use if the organization is not getting the specific support services it needs, while paying for other services that are worthless for the organization's actual needs.

Companies needing such outside IT support should ask for specifics of how the proposed service works in the event of a litigation hold. This will ensure that data is protected while the user is appropriately supported when the triggering event occurs and data needs to be preserved for analysis. There are many suppliers that are engaged for their services based only on a limited cursory review of functionality and a positive sales pitch. This does not need to be the norm.

It is critical that external information processors get the same scrutiny that an internal developer receives when designing a new system, and that shortcuts are avoided in engaging external data processors.

CONTROLLING ELECTRONIC DEVICE INFORMATION— THREE ISSUES

Your Team needs to know about the workings of your systems and associated devices. But it also needs to know how information flows in and out of your system through different types of devices, interacting with the outside electronic world. This is the job of the Chief Information Security Officer, if your organization has an individual with that title or at least that function. The CISO must either be on the Team or work closely with it.

Information Entering Through Company Devices

An organization that understands the treatment of devices in its data inventory, and understands where that data is stored, is in an excellent position to identify the most useful locations from which to collect device data after a hold notice.

An example of this is a central smart phone server, where the information from each company-owned phone is stored and then sent to or received from the phone device. In such a case, you can collect the content of the server to have a complete copy of the content of all company phones without the need to track down each phone individually. Of course this varies among different server software applications. It is also dependent on the promptness of the collection, and whether the phone is dedicated to company use or not.

Obviously this is yet another concern in BYOD environments.

Information Leaving Company Devices

Knowing what information is transferred to portable devices from the system is important, since it is relatively easy to lose those devices. A quick scan of news stories shows that a large number of data breaches are due to the loss of mobile devices. This demonstrates the need to secure mobile devices much more than desktop systems.

It is also important to classify data for security access, so that data which is considered confidential or secret can be restricted to systems that are secure, thereby limiting its distribution.

In many cases, the authorization for access to sensitive information is too widely distributed so that data "leaks" are common and hard to detect.

Unless the company is too small to have more than a skeleton IT staff, at least one member of the IT staff needs to be tasked with information security development (whether or not that person is designated as Chief Information Security Officer), and suitably trained in the many technical issues related to information security. Alternatively, that function needs to be confirmed as part of the services provided by the outside IT service provider. In that way management is appropriately informed both of the scope of unwanted outbound data travel risks, and of ways to prevent such unwanted events. Naturally, an appropriate information security policy includes a continuing program of employee training about data security practices.

In the context of data collection and preservation under a litigation hold, your information security person or CISO is generally a Team resource. In the event the triggering event includes inappropriate data exposure, the information security person is a Team member.

If that function is outsourced, a Team member must be designated during training to coordinate with the outside security personnel, and those personnel need to be aware of the litigation hold concept and process.

Portable Devices: Phones, Laptops, Portable Hard Drives, and Transit Media

As we have mentioned in several contexts, the use of mobile devices complicates control over sensitive information. Company laptops that are not properly monitored by IT between uses are a clear source of concern. Does IT routinely conduct hard-drive examinations after check-in, for indications of unapproved data deletions indicating sensitive company data has been moved away from company control? Are company laptops even checked in and out daily? Or do they freely roam? This can be a serious issue for demonstrating an effective litigation hold and related preservation, to say nothing of data protection itself.

Consider also the indiscriminate use of transit devices such as "flash" or "jump" drives. Exactly what practical control does the company exercise over use of these devices? Is there a policy? Is it actually known to the employees? Has it ever been enforced?

The innovation of using employee devices (BYOD) further complicates the issues of data collection when company information is stored in a device not owned by the company. It is necessary to obtain permission from the device owner to collect device data, or have pre-approved permissions as a condition of appropriate BYOD policies, as discussed in Chapter 5.

All of these raise concerns about the litigation hold, which is inextricably linked to your basic data security program.

DEALING WITH DATA SECURITY AND CLASSIFICATION

It is important for all organizations to understand and identify the information that is sensitive in nature, whether due to regulation, competition and/or privacy reasons. Yet it is surprising how many organizations fail to segregate and limit access to sensitive information in an effective manner. Once you have your data map and data inventory completed (or updated), a thoughtful review of the kinds of data in your systems will reveal much more than your critical trade secrets that is in need of security when a litigation hold data collection is in progress.

Remember, under the Federal Rules your opponent gets to collect data directly from the place where it is stored. That would be the isolated hard drives to which the collected data has been moved for preservation if you prove you used forensically defensible search parameters and collection protocols. If you failed to do an adequate hold, the other side can get a court order allowing them to search your entire universe of systems and devices. If you don't know for sure whether confidential data has been identified and isolated from routine collection under a hold notice, you are more than likely going to let that data out of your control in the course of discovery responses. (By the same token, be prepared to be dumbfounded by the kinds of unwanted data that will come to your litigators and your own forensic consultant from the other side in the same process.)

Here is another example of inadvertent data security failure: the commingling of credit card data with other commercial contract information in a network used by a contractor to manage the air conditioning system. This is your organization's concern as well as your contractor's. Data of these types must be isolated from each other to limit the chance of compromise of sensitive information. Such a compromise can put your organization in the litigation crosshairs for unexpected reasons, when your own data is taken in a data breach at another company. Just as a real-world reminder, a major breach of credit card information at Target Stores came through a prior breach at one of its own service vendors.

Also, as discussed in other contexts, personally identifiable information (PII) such as employee driver's license numbers, social security numbers, medical record numbers, etc. is often contained in databases which are not segregated and protected. This is how that kind of information lands on my desk for forensic analysis as part of a discovery response in litigation.

Data Security Procedures and the Litigation Hold

In today's world, data security and digital forensics are working with each other, because of the need to use digital forensics in determining who is responsible for data breaches.

This merges the analysis of security information with the process of digital collection, particularly in litigation involving intellectual property theft, dissemination of sensitive information and/or theft of secrets.

In such instances the collection of security logs and other similar information is a necessary part of the litigation hold process. The Team must be trained to identify and address this security issue promptly and correctly.

Data Classification—Preserving Value While Preserving Data for Litigation

Previously we mentioned the need to classify sensitive data within a data security process. The classified data becomes inaccessible except through the data security protocol, thus preserving its value to your organization.

This process includes the need to know where classified data is stored in the system. In today's insecure world of information, it is necessary to understand what data is sensitive so that significant effort is made to protect that information.

If this type of information is not truly segregated, and that segregated location identified to the Team, a situation is inadvertently created where supposedly classified data can be collected and then improperly delivered to the litigation opponent.

I have seen examples of HIPPA medical information being released in the process of providing email metadata in a case, and also a case where banking information was released without understanding that it was in the data produced to opposing counsel.

If it is necessary to collect classified information during the litigation hold process, that specialized collected data needs to be segregated from other collected data, so that the parties understand the nature of the data and its importance to the organization. This gives the litigation members of the Team the alert to properly document the terms for restricted access to that data by the other side, including non-disclosure provisions.

DATA SECURITY IN EMPLOYEE-RELATED INCIDENTS

When employees are either voluntarily or involuntarily terminated from the organization, loss of data can occur with or without the intent to do so on either side of the separation. BYOD should come to mind, among other concerns.

It is important that the HR and IT departments work in unison to prevent or mitigate data loss in such circumstances. These departments must also secure any systems or company-owned devices that a terminated employee can still access after workstation privileges are removed.

Voluntary Termination

Even before the firm's going-away party for the employee moving on to a great opportunity elsewhere, or the speech for the retiring one, there needs to be a plan in place dealing with data security for the system and all devices, with the check-off list in HR's to-do folder.

Company-Owned Devices: Collection and Inspection

In the case of a voluntary termination, it is still important to collect all company- owned devices such as laptop computers, smart phones, tablets and other devices from the employee in advance of the final day of work, along with collecting access badges, etc. as the employee leaves for the last time.

If the devices are going to be redeployed either immediately or in due course, as is the case in most organizations, and the employee holds a key position in the organization or has access to any classified data, or has been a key player in a triggering event, then we recommend that the contents of the departing employee's devices be collected forensically before any device redeployment, in case of future litigation involving actions by that employee. A Fortune 500 client has the policy that when anyone holding a position of Director or higher leaves the company, regardless of the reason, the employee's devices are automatically imaged. This limits later effort trying to recreate the device's data from secondary sources such as backups, or copies in other locations.

During a voluntary termination, it is important to collect the company-owned mobile devices prior to the last day of work, so that there is time to verify that the devices have not been erased or tampered with. Not every voluntary termination occurs with the best intentions towards the employer. And discovering that key information has been deleted from a company-owned device can be an unpleasant surprise, and a very expensive one, if it is necessary to recover the data due to a breach, non-compete agreements or the transfer of sensitive data.

The authors have observed cases where an employee hands in a computer on the last day of work and it is completely empty of all data, with the excuse is that he had personal information in the system that he did not want to share with the next employee. Or, the case where the executive-level employee insisted that the laptop's hard drive crashed a few days previously, destroying a significant quantity of competition-sensitive information. Later forensic imaging showed that a commercial program to completely erase the contents of a drive had been run on the drive—seven times! The ex-executive's explanation was not as well received in the non-compete lawsuit as the forensic analyst's.

It is important for the organization to have policies, acknowledged by all employees, that specify the procedures that will be used in handling electronic devices upon termination, as well as what happens to devices that are to be redeployed to new employees.

Additionally, the policy should be clear that personal information placed on company-owned computers and other devices is accessible by the company, and that there is no presumption of privacy in connection with any such computer or other device. Employees using company computers or other devices to post to social media should be required to periodically confirm that they know there is a "no privacy" policy.

Employee-Owned Devices at Voluntary Termination

In the case of employee-owned devices in a BYOD environment, a company must have a clear inspection policy plus a written agreement signed by each employee in order to collect information from the employee's devices. There is no consistency in the rules about this practice from one geographic area to another. But in most cases the employee can refuse to allow such data access or copying by the employer in the absence of such a signed agreement. In other cases the employee can remove data from a device and claim there is no data in it at the time of request, and the employer is powerless to prove otherwise.

If the company is not ready to take on the rigors of BYOD, it should not allow employees to access sensitive company data and control it on personal devices.

If the company has adequate policies, rigorously enforced, then a properly-collected image of the mobile device is the prudent route to take, to preserve the content in case of future disputes.

Involuntary Termination Scenarios

Involuntary termination comes in many forms, from the firing for cause of a dishonest employee, to department-wide or company-wide reduction in force (RIF) for economic reasons, to corporate mergers, to spin-offs of corporate divisions. Each of these has a different "temperature" in terms of employer-employee relations. In dealing with data security and system/device control, getting the temperature right and handling the system and device data issue properly will save problems later.

In any case of involuntary termination of more than one or two employees, whether RIF, spin-off, or other situation, the company needs to develop a situation-appropriate data-control plan in advance of announcing the forthcoming event.

In such corporate structural events, collection of all corporate data is necessary to preserve it during the structural transition, so that the appropriate data ends up at the appropriate location after the transition is complete. Parenthetically, this is the obvious time for a carefully documented system-wide data map and data inventory, to eliminate later disputes over data access and completeness.

A good example is when an operating unit is sold to another enterprise. The data owner wants to preserve the information as of the transfer date, while the computers and servers of the operating unit will be transferred to the new owner, along with a copy of the data for reference to past transactions. Control of the data, and assurances of completeness, are important to both parties.

The more traditional involuntary termination situation, of course, is when an individual employee is terminated for cause and there is a likelihood of future litigation.

Termination of Access to the System and Other Devices

In involuntary terminations, whether structural or for cause, it is necessary to terminate each individual employee's access to both the computer system and to devices containing company data, in advance of the termination notice. This is to prevent the removal or corruption of data (which may later be evidence) by the employee.

In many cases, the data collection is conducted in a clandestine fashion in order to preserve evidence supporting civil or criminal actions against the suspect.

Another example is the termination of a network administrator. In such a case, the employee about to be terminated has the highest-level access to all the data in the company's servers and devices. It is generally considered prudent to designate the successor administrator, and put the prior administrator on immediate leave (with or without any necessary pretexts to prevent tampering). Then the previous employee's administrative credentials are terminated prior to his return from leave. IT then conducts a complete collection and examination of all data on the administrator's assigned computers as quickly as possible, so that the new administrator can quickly take control of network operations and system downtime is minimized.

Collection of Company-Owned Devices at Involuntary Terminations

All company-owned devices need to be collected prior to involuntary termination, or suspension for cause of an employee. Once again, we have seen a multitude of cases where the employee removes all data from company devices (whether by destroying the data or by moving it to another device) prior to turning them over to the company.

If the employee has engaged in inappropriate behavior, this serves to cover his tracks, at least in the short term. But note that it does not exonerate the company from legal claims for the period when he was its employee.

In the case of RIF, merger, or other structural reasons for the involuntary termination, honest and frequent communication about the matter will help to minimize bad acts by departing employees. Collection and inspection of company devices can be handled in a reasonably straightforward way, by cooperative protocols managed by IT and the network administrator, if employees perceive that they are being treated in a fair and respectful manner on their way out the door. If the mass terminations are handled badly, device theft and associated data destruction are among the many likely data-related bad outcomes for the company.

Data Deletion from BYOD Devices

While there is danger that the involuntarily-terminated employee will wipe company devices, there is also danger that employees will take sensitive company information out of the organization's control in their own personal devices. I recall a case in which the employer did not want to purchase laptops for employees' business use, because of "accidents" that required replacement of units from time to time. The company instituted a BYOD policy without written access agreements. In that case, the employer was then sued by a third party over the actions of two employees who were terminated for cause. It took significant expense in legal and forensic consultant fees and court time to arrive at a negotiated settlement, because the former employees refused to turn over their personal computers. In that case a litigation hold and associated preservation could provide only an inaccurate and partial evidentiary picture of the triggering event, defeating any possible factual defense by the company.

Could this scenario have been avoided by an access-to-inspect agreement? Perhaps or perhaps not. Could it have been avoided by a complete access agreement, allowing the company to electronically access the laptop at any time to inspect (and preserve) its contents? Again, perhaps or perhaps not. The company's failure to even contemplate the downside of BYOD made that discussion academic in the end, when the employees acted against the company's interests and the company was powerless to protect itself.

Special Personnel with Special Privileges

In the case of executives, IT personnel, or other specialized employees with special computer system privileges, such as access to classified, highly-sensitive information and other special data, the organization must carefully structure written access authorizations. These will allow the organization to collect and preserve ESI to protect sensitive information in a cost-effective manner, while respecting the employee's privacy. Most individuals in these roles are professionals. They can be treated as such in establishing understandings on what occurs if the employee wants to separate from the organization, or the organization wants the employee to leave in a non-accusatory situation.

As we have noted before, it's all about prior strategic thinking, good Team training, and having the elements of the data-control plan in effect when the Team is needed.

CHAPTER 9

The Cloud and Other Complexities

In this chapter, we will look briefly at some technically complex issues related to data preservation, including The Cloud and certain complex data environments.

CLOUD COMPUTING

Cloud computing has come on the scene in the past few years as a way of purchasing computing resources in the same manner that the company purchases services from utilities, such as electricity and water. The obvious attraction of this form of computing is that the user can purchase computing resources on demand, as and when needed, and also dispose of excess resources as and when needed.

For example, a company that has a retail website can purchase web server demand capacity based on its customer demand hours. As more customers connect, additional web server capacity is automatically available to meet the users' needs. Once the user traffic begins to slow down in the daily cycle, the additional resources can be released and, accordingly, the charges for those additional resources stop. These access operations can be automated, so that specific programmed triggers are calling and releasing resources as necessary any time of day or night.

Cloud services come in various forms, based on the degree to which the Cloud user wishes to engage in the management of the Cloud environment. There are three different Cloud service levels: Infrastructure as a Service (IaaS), Platform as a Service (PaaS), and Software as a Service (SaaS). These Cloud service levels are further explained in their respective sections below.

In addition, Cloud services include what are termed "software-defined networks." These networks develop in the same manner as the Cloud services themselves, on demand, and are reconfigured on demand as necessary, contrary to traditional networks which are made up of physical components, routers and switches.

109

Regardless of the model selected, the user is responsible for actually reading the terms of service and understanding exactly what the Cloud service provider will, and more importantly will not, provide. Unsuspecting users have been shocked to find out in a crisis that their Cloud service provider has no obligation to back up stored data.

Consider the physical facts about the "Cloud"—your provider's Cloud is actually a large series of linked servers, often called a server farm, physically located in a building somewhere, typically in part of a large office building or warehouse park that is no longer attractive as office space. The service provider may have server farms scattered throughout the country, and perhaps throughout several countries. Other providers have server farms similarly located.

For each server farm, that building, like buildings everywhere, is subject to the effects of local disasters such as fire, flood, tornadoes in the Midwest, hurricanes along the Gulf Coast, earthquakes on the Pacific Coast, extreme weather events everywhere, etc. Obviously, those disaster-related effects can include loss of electric power, rising water within a building, and other such unhappy events. That is not the moment for you to find out that your contract has no provision requiring your provider to back up any of your data or otherwise make any particular effort to preserve it in the event of perfectly forseeable "act of God" events.

Also, find out in advance whether your tiny portion of the Cloud is even going to be within the United States. Read the contract, not the marketing brochure. You will in the course of the litigation receive your opponent's request that you instruct your provider to allow access to inspect documents under the Rules. That is not the moment to find out your Cloud is in Ireland (where, incidentally, a lot of email and social media servers are located—see Chapter 12), where information access is highly restricted by both local law and European Union privacy laws.

We've said it before. We'll say it again. Never Assume!

Cloud Service Models
IaaS—Infrastructure as a Service
The IaaS Cloud service model provides the closest comparison to a physical network that can be purchased in the Cloud service world.

An IaaS can be part of a public or private Cloud environment, or a combination known as a hybrid Cloud.

In an IaaS, the service provider gives the user access to a console that enables the user to create a logical-based computing environment with servers, storage, databases, and other functions. This environment operates in the same manner as a physical computer room would, providing the applications and data necessary to run the organization.

The main difference between your own computer room and the IaaS is that the IaaS user does not have control over the actual hardware, cables and other network devices providing the services. Rather, you only have "control" over their virtual equivalents.

Additionally, the virtual server users are sharing the physical hardware with multiple other organizations. This is what is referred to as a public Cloud. The same can be accomplished in a private Cloud, where the physical Cloud at one server center is dedicated to only one customer.

There are substantial risks involved in operating in a shared environment, particularly if the boundaries between users are not clearly defined and strictly enforced. IaaS environments can be programmed to automatically add and delete resources based on the user's changing needs. Some examples of businesses operating in an IaaS environment are Amazon.com©, Facebook©, and Windows Live©.

There are limitations on the degree of control the user can exercise in an IaaS environment, including limits on the ability to collect and preserve data in support of litigation and investigations. In most instances, the user is dependent on the Cloud provider to collect data, and more importantly to properly document that collection. The collection will take place from the portions of the devices assigned from time to time to the user, by individuals who may have little or no forensic training, with little or no supervision from forensic consultants, attorneys and other responsible parties.

This easily creates situations in which it is extremely difficult to ascertain the accuracy or completeness of the data collected—the unavoidable opposite of the desired situation with the Team's litigation hold preservation procedure. The provider's sales and marketing people are unlikely to know the answers to hold-related questions. Check the terms of service. Ask now, not later.

PaaS—Platform as a Service
In the PaaS level of service, the Cloud provider delivers space on a logical server to run an application designed by the user.

In this case, for example, an organization that wants to develop a mobile application would outsource all the operating and administrative requirements of the computing environment to the Cloud, and only control the programming and user interface portions of the task. This simplifies the need for specialized technical help in the start-up phase of a new enterprise.

The issues of collecting litigation-related ESI from PaaS Cloud-based resources for preservation under the litigation hold are similar to those of IaaS, in that the Cloud provider has total control over the process of data collection from the files used by the developer's application. This problem can be circumvented if the developer has, for example, programmed an interface to collect each application user's data individually.

But data such as network and administrative commands, and other areas not in the control of the Cloud user, would have to be collected by the Cloud provider, if available. This creates an even greater level of reliance on the Cloud provider to support its customer. That reliance may be misplaced. The provider's sales and marketing people are unlikely to know.... Check the terms of service. Ask now, not later.

SaaS—Software as a Service

SaaS is the sale of an application on a subscription basis—applications that previously had to be purchased and installed on a local physical server or workstation. There are many examples of this type of product: MS Office©, Salesforce.com©, GoToMeeting©, Google Mail©, VoIP© phone services, Photoshop©, and many more.

The primary attraction of the SaaS level of service is that it transfers the responsibility for software maintenance to a third party. This can be effective where there are limited human resources in the IT department, or in a highly distributed organization with many small business units.

In the SaaS case, however, the provider has total control, and can change the software at any time to add or delete features, fixes, or operation of the product, generally without notice to or approval (or objection) by the end user.

In choosing to employ a SaaS environment, it is critical to understand the limitations of data collection features. Procedures for requesting the equivalent of the litigation hold and associated collection and preservation in a timely manner may be cumbersome or ineffective. Check the terms of service. The provider's sales and marketing people are unlikely to know.... Ask now, not later. (If you are sensing an echo here, you should be writing something on your hand.)

Forensic Limitations and Challenges of Cloud Computing

Cloud computing presents a unique challenge to the forensic data collections process that has been developed during the past 15 years.

The primary reason is that traditional digital forensic practices are based on the collection of data from physical devices, such as memory, hard drives, servers, etc., at specific physical locations. When confronted with the Cloud environment that provides virtual services to numerous clients, the forensic consultant cannot image data in a traditional forensic method as used in a physical environment that only contains one client's data. If the traditional method were used in the Cloud, it would inappropriately collect the data of many other users as part of the image.

In some cases, Cloud storage is spread over a number of storage application server locations, serving thousands of Cloud users, with the data simply identified in a way that presents the viewer with a logical storage unit associated with the user. In reality, the data next to any particular portion of the user's data on the servers could belong to an organization on another continent.

These unique problems of data storage methods, processor unitization and assignment have led many large Cloud users to demand what are commonly called private Clouds. In this case, the Cloud hardware environment of a specific server group is dedicated to one Cloud user. This limits the potential commingling of data from another organization with the client's data. In addition, the features of security and redundancy can be more closely controlled than in a public Cloud. Predictably, a private Cloud is not cheap.

As we have reminded you before, the litigation hold collection process may not be possible under your terms of service, or proper procedures may be financially prohibitive. Ask now, not later.

COMPLEX ENVIRONMENTS

The world of computing continues to evolve in direct correlation to the advances in hardware and in computing power. The evolution of equipment, software, services, systems and approaches continues to increase efficiency and lower the need for resources in delivering user services. Here are some of these emerging technologies that you may wish to follow as your own organization's needs develop. Each has its own ESI-preservation challenges.

Software Defined Networks

"Software Defined Networks" is the term for use of software to dynamically deliver network services on a demand basis. This is independent of the constraints caused by the development cycles of networking vendors' hardware, and of traditional networking environments.

These networks allow for the allocation of bandwidth on a demand basis, to accommodate the high volume applications in use today (for example, delivery of entertainment programming, Big Data analysis, etc.).

Big Data

"Big Data" is, simply, extremely high data flow, whether from a single source (that streaming movie video) or multiple sources (such as micro-units in a manufacturing facility producing huge data flows through various controllers). Big Data has been in discussion among IT professionals for many years. Now that Cloud computing can enlist computing capacity on a demand basis, it is possible to dynamically use the resources without having to anticipate the size of server clusters needed to process the data.

This coupling of Cloud computing's dynamic capacity and Big Data volume promises to develop new ways of analyzing information for anomalies, such as to solve the proverbial needle in the haystack problem. Big Data computing processes can be applied to large data sets to find information patterns useful to a particular user. These information patterns will help decision makers focus resources on those portions of the data that need a higher level of analysis.

In addition, this high-volume/high speed process will uncover patterns in the data that could not be seen previously, due to the large volume of data points to review.

This, coupled with the Internet of Things concept, will allow for the analysis of weather patterns, equipment failure reporting in complex industrial settings, health trends, etc.

Internet of Things

The "Internet of Things" (IoT) is the application of miniaturized single-use devices to measure a specific type of reading (for example, temperature, pressure, vibration, light, etc.). We are not just talking about the computer in your company's delivery trucks (and your car), with the WiFi capability that can update the vehicle's systems remotely.

These devices are designed to communicate over low power networks, transmitting their information to a collection point device. That device forwards the data packets to a data repository, where Big Data computing techniques are applied to reveal unique patterns and trends in the data from many micro-sources.

IoT will revolutionize the manner in which information is collected and processed to understand trends and shape decisions based on them.

IT'S ALL HAPPENING RIGHT NOW

These complex environments are not in the future. They are occurring now. Organizations you know about are using them. Your Team needs to be aware of these environments' existence before the triggering event occurs and you go into "hold" mode. Team members should be ready to make appropriate inquiries and effectively capture data that should be of concern to your organization. And, of course, that applies equally when you are inquiring of your opponent's attorneys about their hold procedures.

CHAPTER 10

Putting it All Together: When the First Alarm Sounds, Hold It!

THE CRITICAL MOMENT TO BEGIN PRESERVATION

The Team members have been identified and received training in how the Team is going to function, including their individual responsibilities. Scenarios for likely events have been discussed within the Team, based on industry-wide litigation statistics. Table exercises for those scenarios have been completed. The company's employee handbook has been updated to let everyone know the Team exists, including the proper way to contact the Team liaison in case of a triggering event.

Then it happens—maybe an accident involving the company's personnel or property. Maybe an employee is suspected of theft of the company's intellectual property. Maybe a notice arrives from the Equal Employment Opportunity Commission of a claim for employment discrimination by a female former executive. The Team leaders recognize it for what it is—a triggering event. Now what?

Preservation Responsibilities—Avoiding the Fatal Pre-Litigation Error

There is not a specific section or paragraph in the Federal Rules that states the pre-litigation ESI hold requirement. It was developed through case law, not by rule-making. However, Rule 37(e) points out that your organization is in trouble in several ways if you haven't preserved relevant ESI after finding out about a triggering event, as we discussed in Chapter 2.

Remember, the litigation hold duty to preserve data begins at the moment a reasonable person would think a lawsuit would be likely in the future about that event. The duty does not begin at the moment the lawsuit arrives on General Counsel's desk. Not the moment the judge signs the preliminary discovery scheduling order, two months into the lawsuit. Not the moment six months into pretrial document production when litigation counsel admits to the judge that no hold notice was ever sent to the key players to save ESI. Now. As soon

115

CONTENTS

as a reasonably suspicious mind would say the word "lawyers." (And we note, not a paranoid person, just a reasonably experienced adult in your industry.)

Write it on your hand. At the moment you know, spread the word: HOLD IT.

Simple test, Team members: Would you, reasonably informed adults, expect legal trouble under the circumstances you have just found out about? Then this is the moment when the litigation hold notice needs to be drafted, refined, and sent to everyone who might be connected to an ESI data custodian or key player (including those who were connected to one at the time of the triggering event).

It is critical for you to think broadly. HR can shine here. It is smarter to notify everyone who has been in a working group since before the event, rather than to skip two or three critical people that the working group knows are connected to the event. HR can also help find former employees who may have useful information about the working group's actual data-handling practices.

The hold notice clearly instructs every one of the key players and their associated data custodians to be ready to assist IT to segregate and save all ESI of everyone that might even possibly be related to the incident, for at least a preliminary review. Just as an example from our painful experience, be sure everyone understands about NOT putting ANY emails in the delete folder until they have been sorted. And, obviously, no one should empty any folders, on any device.

We are not offering you any "form" hold notices, for the simple reason that every triggering event, every group of key players, every organizational structure is different. It would be an extreme disservice for us to suggest that there is a "one size fits all" hold notice, or even a small group of them. In our experience, time spent looking for the perfect form, or looking for one from a different situation, is time wasted. You will find many legal blogs with suggestions for the contents of the notice. Please feel free to use the ideas that fit a particular event, and ignore the ones that don't. Before disaster strikes, write a few variants of your own "form" within the Team, to suit your own organization and its own litigation history. You'll be safer in the long run. And, of course, you'll have it in the "Hold Notice Forms" folder when the alarm sounds.

When the alarm does sound, if you are more than a few days out from the actual occurrence of the triggering event, IT needs to immediately attend to the deleted items/trash folders as key players are being notified to preserve, and if necessary retrieve data. And, as Chapter 2 made painfully clear, IT needs to temporarily stop all automatic data pruning functions in all systems.

While the identification of key players and notice drafting is in progress, IT members of the team must quickly deal with the computer system's auto-delete maintenance functions, and locate every portable device related to each of the key players.

Then, collect, collect, collect, using the protocols developed with your forensic consultant's guidance. And, of course, alert the consultant to be on stand-by.

The consultant will already have trained the IT members of the Team about careful documentation, reflecting the Team's thoughtful approach to collection. The documentation operates as what in the CSI world is referred to as chain of custody and authentication. This means simply that the metadata associated with each electronic file is accurately preserved with the document. When and if the electronic document is offered as evidence at trial, your litigation counsel can prove that the document as presented is exactly as it was at the moment of the triggering event. In other words the electronic file now, at the moment of preservation, is the precise document offered in the future—same author, same creation and editing data, same everything. From the lawyer's perspective, the document can be evidence acceptable under Federal Rule of Evidence 901 or its state law equivalent. Its accuracy can be relied on by the judge and jury.

After all the ESI is collected from every conceivable source and segregated to temporary storage, and after the forensic protocols have been documented in detail, you can reorganize the Team to identify and organize the real evidence captured by the hold.

Then you can quickly release the rest of the key players' ESI back to regular ESI maintenance, without creating a storage and maintenance nightmare.

Key Players—Revisiting the Concept

For this preliminary phase, save all ESI generated by or received by two kinds of "key players"—(1) the obvious "participant" key players, individuals who are likely to be called as witnesses based on their business functions and likely participation in the triggering event, plus (2) their associated "custodian" group of supervisors and support staff, including secretaries, assistants, active subordinates, supervised interns, etc. Individuals in the second group may be custodians of ESI, because they are likely to have communicated with participant key players, or created or managed ESI for them. The first group is of particular interest to the lawyers on the Team. The second group is of greatest interest to the Team's IT members. All of them should be identifiable by HR.

By capturing ESI from both groups at the start, you will have a wide enough scope to pick up ESI related to participant key players who do not generate 100% of their own documents and communications, and who undoubtedly don't manage data clean-up for their documents and communications. At the beginning you are looking for all the custodians plus the participants.

Don't worry about data volume at this stage. Temporary storage is cheap, and you already have some external storage capacity stashed in the IT department just for this occasion.

Since you've already prepared for this and have your forensic consultant's electronic tools in your system, you'll be doing the initial identification by way of a focused group of search terms centered on all the custodians. These are the terms the Team is developing under the supervision of your forensics consultant. The IT members of the Team just need to be ahead of the auto-delete functions of your software at this stage.

You also have identified the widest group of people who need to be alerted not to view, change or delete ESI associated with the triggering event, and if possible to retrieve recently deleted ESI. These are key players, both participants and custodians, who need to be alerted immediately by the team's forensics/IT members, for preservation tagging by IT at the auto-delete level of the computer system, as well as for alerts to avoid manual deleting.

Note that some of the key players may no longer be associated with the working group or even the company, whether they were reassigned or transferred, or were voluntarily or involuntarily separated from their relationship as employees, contractors, consultants, etc. But the contents of their computers and other devices should still be available.

For ESI custodians who have been reassigned to other positions, but who know about a former key player's ESI, be certain they are included in the hold notice group. The notice goes to the real-world people who are in actual control of the ESI you need, and those no longer in control who know where it is. The hold notice distribution list needs careful vetting by HR for the non-obvious.

Speaking of distribution of the hold notice, there is no such thing as an effective litigation-hold notice that doesn't get to the key players and custodians, the people who control or know about the ESI in the real world. A federal judge will be glad to point this deficiency out in painful detail to litigation counsel, in-house counsel and senior management if you don't think that concept is important. It is your Team's job to make them look good (the usual employee's job) by being certain they don't have that particular bad experience on your watch. You don't need to repeat some of the "case nibbles" from Chapter 2 involving the fallout from hold notices that only went to a few senior managers and no one else.

A GREAT QUESTION THAT HAS ALREADY BEEN ANSWERED FOR YOU

We assume you are now muttering under your breath, along the lines of "That's easy for you to say, writers. You already know how to do this stuff." You are entirely right, we do know the punchline. And we're here to share it with you, in two parts.

The Sedona Conference®

The Sedona Conference is a non-profit, non-partisan thinktank based in Arizona. It is composed of various working groups focused on specific topics, but with the overall aim to define best practices in specific areas of law, and to develop practical solutions to challenges which impede development of excellence in American and international legal practice.

The Sedona Conference has been active in developing specific practical steps in reasonable and defensible electronic discovery. One of its early products was the "Sedona Conference Cooperation Proclamation," which has been adopted by and cited by numerous courts. From its first edition in 2004 to its current iteration, it has reflected the efforts of judges, practicing trial lawyers, and others to move the evidence discovery process toward the Rule 1 requirements of cooperation and proportionality.

Numerous papers from Working Group 1 (Electronic Document Retention and Production) are available on the Sedona Conference website (see our Resources Appendix). These include detailed and practical instructions about all aspects of electronic evidence, from the litigation hold to "possession, custody, or control" of ESI in the Cloud and other similar topics.

The Sedona Conference, through Kenneth J. Withers, is also a co-author of "Electronic Discovery and Digital Evidence Cases and Materials" (3d ed., West Academic, 2015), with Judge Shira A. Scheindlin (yes, that Judge Scheindlin) and Professor Daniel J. Capra of Fordham University School of Law. As its name indicates, this is a law school text. The third edition includes materials related to the 2015 Rules amendments as well as updates on fast-changing practices such as technology-assisted review in discovery.

International Organization for Standardization (ISO)

ISO/IEC 27050-3.2, Annex A—Sample questions for identification of ESI.

That is the designation of the working draft of a document we are particularly fond of. It is being prepared by the International Organization for Standardization (ISO), through various technical working groups. It is titled "Information technology—Security techniques—Electronic discovery—Part 3: Code of practice for electronic discovery." Annex A is a complete set of questions for your Team to use in identifying the custodian key players, by finding the people who are knowledgeable about data repositories, records management, system elements, etc. It includes all the questions the Team should ask each of those individuals.

ISO is an international organization formed to identify best practices in thousands of areas, including information security and electronic evidence procedures. Its members are the agencies of national governments tasked with standardizing practices in industries as well as professions around the world.

The official U.S. member of ISO is the National Institute of Standards and Technology (NIST). Among the participants in NIST's working group are the American Bar Association's Electronic Discovery and Digital Evidence (EDDE) Committee, and many other interested groups and individuals.

ISO/IEC document 27050 is one of a group of related documents (27037-27050) concerning digital evidence collection, preservation, analysis and production. ISO 27037 was finalized in 2012, and is designated "Guidelines for identification, collection, acquisition and preservation of digital evidence." ISO 27042 was published in final form in 2015, and is designated "Guidelines for the analysis and interpretation of digital evidence."

This group of documents, taken together, constitutes the thinking of digital evidence experts (lawyers as well as forensics professionals) from around the world. Its purpose is to identify and promote best practices in the area of e-discovery. Predictably, it is a dynamic set of documents, as both technology and legal practices develop around the world.

Put your bookmark here and go look at our Resources Appendix for the websites of both the Sedona Conference and ISO. It will improve your outlook about this entire process. Each site contains a wealth of detail about the many arcane nooks and crannies of ESI preservation and e-discovery.

IDENTIFYING THE SCOPE OF THE PRESERVATION HOLD BY COMMUNICATING WITHIN THE TEAM

Identifying this initial, wider "hold" group of custodian key players gives you the best opportunity to think early about appropriate strategies, and to gather the widest possible universe of information about the triggering event.

Why worry about the widest possible universe of information? Because the worst possible source of critical information about the triggering event is your opponent, whether in a courtroom or in settlement negotiations. Bad preservation can equal a bad outcome. Sloppy thinking guarantees bad preservation. Your sole reason for existence as a Team is so your company's management can accurately understand the entire narrative surrounding the triggering event before there is any contact with anyone else.

Putting it another way, effective and prompt initial action avoids later problems with analyzing risk exposure. The first step on the path to knowing the whole story is a well-thought-out hold and associated preservation program, well executed, so your Team's management members can understand the actual risk level of any event-related litigation and respond appropriately.

This is also the moment for the Team leaders to control impulsive actions within the Team as well as within management, other IT personnel, and the larger organization. In the early stages after a triggering event, knowledge is your weapon. The watchphrase can only be "Think, Ask, Then Hold It!"

Avoid letting anyone on the Team jump to conclusions before the facts can speak for themselves. You cannot give your litigation, risk management and negotiation managers a defensible narrative to work from if you, the Team members, don't collect, analyze and convey the whole story. You, the Team members, are tasked with finding out the whole truth, so don't let anyone on the team (or anyone else in management) decide what the narrative and strategy should be in the absence of all the facts.

From a forensic as well as legal perspective, Team members need to remind all affected employees, key players and other custodians alike, to avoid contamination or destruction of metadata. The essential distinction between an electronic document and a physical document is the electronic history of creation and development of an electronic file—its metadata. You need to know that you have preserved the integrity of each electronic document, not least for your own analytical purposes, long before the other side sees a single electronic document.

At this early stage, the hold notice must be both clear and emphatic on this point. No one, repeat no one, other than Team members should look at or in any other way "help" identify and collect ESI. Don't let untrained "helpful" people (however well-intentioned) contaminate or corrupt this critical information by allowing sloppy handling of ESI. This includes such unhelpful actions as copying ESI files from their original locations to a new folder, and other movement of files from their original locations.

The idle busybody or the employee in search of a little power is your worst enemy at this moment. Make sure the hold notice is emphatic on this point. Team members as well as key players and other custodians should be specifically instructed NOT to create inappropriate metadata, by indiscriminately and/or repeatedly opening electronic files or trying to inspect the content of "hot" memos, or moving files around in the system. Be plain--nothing, without forensic/IT supervision.

Also, as you and the other Team members are dashing around to get things stabilized, remember that many aspects of software that are your friends in the everyday world of work are your enemies in data collection. For example, your word-processing software probably has a handy auto-dating function when you draft a memo or letter. Great, no? Emphatically no at this point, when several "helpful" employees open the original electronic file to see if there's anything interesting in there, and thereby change the date several times on the stored document.

Develop and enforce an inspection protocol using copied files for key players to review in connection with your ESI search-terms. Don't let the helpful types inspect anything without forensic/IT supervision.

Putting it another way, don't carelessly kill your own case. Alert all key players and other custodians immediately. Remind them to contact IT rather than take it upon themselves to do what needs to be done. Their job is solely to avoid deleting or changing ESI—nothing else. Job number one: Make sure they understand that. Job number two: Make sure they remember that.

The Litigation Hold Notice—Think Carefully, Act Quickly

We saw in Chapter 2 how easily a litigation hold notice can go off the rails—never sent at all, sent to only three people instead of seventy-five, vague beyond all comprehension—you remember the stories.

This is the moment to think, and draft, carefully. This is, in effect, a verbal fire alarm going out to your own side, to act in a specific way, immediately.

Remember the elementary school exercise in news writing? Use it now. Who, what, when, where, why, how and whatever else is needed to give a complete and accurate verbal picture of the situation. But briefly. The notice is an instruction, not a scholarly analysis.

You need to identify the triggering event, plus the key players, so that they and their associated supervisors, support-staff and other custodians can act (including assisting each other). They need to know that the whole point is to preserve evidence, without touching it in any way. They may not be CSI fans, but they know the concept. Tell them whom to contact, immediately, on the tech side of the Team, if they think anything is already in jeopardy (emails in the delete bin, working document folders recently emptied, etc.).

Make it clear that they are not to inspect ESI, not to be "helpful" without direct instructions, not to do anything themselves with ESI, and most especially not to start opening files to see if something might be "evidence." Make it plain, politely, that at this point curiosity and misplaced "helpfulness" will get them in very big trouble.

Communicating From the Team to the Rest of the Organization—No Surprises

Did you really think no one in your organization would notice a triggering event? Trust us, it was the topic of serious gossip in the break room long before management got the head's up. So respond accordingly. Make the people who know useful things be useful to you—the expanded key players' list.

The Team should be directly contacting every key player (including all the custodians in the wider group) as quickly as possible, to be sure they are onboard with the plan as outlined in the notice, and ready to assist in identifying and preserving ESI the second they get the hold notice. This eliminates the nasty surprise when the Team belatedly discovers that the intellectual-property thief, on his way out the door with the security team, reminded his secretary and assistant to clear out all his "old" email folders under the company's documents retention policy. Or the secretary who was transferred from a key player's support staff to another assignment around the time of the triggering event, and who knows much more than you thought about someone's documents practices. To say nothing of wandering electronic devices. Don't ignore the HR members of your team—their knowledge of personnel movements is critical.

AFTER THE NOTICE: EXECUTING THE HOLD AND PRESERVING ESI FOR ANALYSIS

You now have a group of employees sitting around wondering if they can touch their workstations, laptops, tablets and smart phones. It's IT's turn to lead.

Isolating Electronic Devices and Storing Data— CIO and IT's Roles

The process of ESI preservation is fraught with procedural mistakes, errors in judgment and missed opportunities. Generally, organizations that do not rehearse this a few times and fine-tune their procedures make errors frequently. Occasionally, by missed signals and oversights, they make fatal errors, so critical evidence is destroyed.

Once the key players and other custodians holding the ESI are identified and alerted by the litigation hold notice, the next step is to for the forensic/IT side of the Team to develop a list of the specific types of data files to be collected from each custodian's contributions to the computer system and devices. This is generally done in groups of files so as to limit the amount of analysis time spent in fine detail; it is easier and better to over-collect than under-collect at this point.

There are many tools commercially available for collection of files from desktops and servers. If your organization has a tool like (merely for example, without endorsing) Access Technologies' product FTK Enterprise® or the Encase Enterprise® version, the digital forensics team will get a list of custodians and collect all data files from their respective machines, server files and folders, mailboxes, etc.

Once collected, these files are then culled by time brackets that pertain to the triggering event. They are then de-duplicated and finally run against the NIST known-file database to eliminate stock documents that have no preservation value.

Analyzing Electronic Information—Your Digital Forensic Consultant's Role

The digital forensic consultant's role in the process of collection is to devise the most efficient and cost effective plan for conducting the collection, and parsing the information to retain what is valuable for the legal Team members to review through technology-assisted review. The collection plan changes from organization to organization, because circumstances are different in each. It changes from event to event for the same reason. What is important is that someone who has the skills to understand the complete process will serve as the point of reference when the collection-preservation-analysis process is ongoing, so that handling and analysis errors are minimized.

The individual can be an internal employee or an outside consultant, depending on your organization's size. But it is crucial that a high level of technical knowledge and forensic data protocol training are present from the beginning, to advise, devise, implement, and supervise the data collection and later analysis. Ambitious amateurs need not apply.

STORING ESI IS CHEAP—STOP ROUTINE STORAGE/DESTRUCTION PROCEDURES ASAP

In the 21st century the cost of ESI storage is pennies per Gigabyte, in some cases less than 5 cents per GB, unlike late 20th century situations. Therefore the cost is now very small to store large quantities of ESI in separate storage. It only makes sense, therefore, to have some serious external storage capacity stashed in IT's work area, just to lower the general craziness level when the alarm sounds.

Once the desired ESI has been collected and moved to separate storage, the working storage routine of the company is freed up to continue running operations normally. The sooner this can happen, the lower the anxiety level will be for the rest of management and IT, and the easier it will be for your Team members to deal with them.

Your IT department should have already reviewed their data destruction policies, to determine whether their current approach and scope are appropriate or in need of updating. In many cases, data destruction parameters are left over from the days when data storage was expensive, and a Gigabyte would cost over $1, to say nothing of physical storage demands. Those days are over.

In addition, thoughtful use of Cloud-based storage can represent an economical alternative to store the collected files held for potential litigation. We discussed Cloud issues in Chapter 9, so that you already have a clear view of the upside and downside of reliance on the Cloud when making evidence-storage decisions.

COMMUNICATION BETWEEN COUNSEL—THE TEAM AND EFFECTIVE USE OF RULES 26 & 34

Let's stop a moment for a reality check. There is unlikely to be any justification for the expense of long-term storage for 26 Terabytes of ESI for a $50,000 case. There is every point in saving 26 Terabytes of information for a $50,000,000 case.

This is proportionality. It's why the inside members of the Team, notably including risk management, need to be in early contact with experienced litigation counsel after a triggering event, to get a preliminary assessment of the actual scope of the likely financial claim.

Naturally, as the cost-to-size ratio for external electronic storage goes down, the amount of ESI you would reasonably be expected to save will change. No judge will be amused by the proposition that you didn't save the ESI related to a particular issue or key player because an additional external hard drive would cost $200. The judge will understand if you didn't save all the duplicates of an email message and all the drafts of a document if the cost would be $10,000 on a claim of $50,000.

Proportionality—keep it in mind when someone in management is having a melt-down about an over-enthusiastic discovery demand from the other side. The Team is ready to handle it.

Proportionality also means the legal members of the Team need to keep the evidence discovery process on a short leash, by enforcing the limits ordered by amended Rules 26 and 34. Remember, 15 requests for ESI documents does not mean 15 vague and generic requests, each of which has 120 subparts.

The point of the Rules amendments is to put an end to gamesmanship and "litigating the opponent into bankruptcy." A well-thought-out response, informed by good forensic advice, will handle many tactics that are politely referred to in the courthouse hallways as "motion to over-reach."

And by the same token, your own discovery requests need to be focused as well. Bye-bye to the canned sets of requests for documents, to be cranked out by a law clerk. Give your litigation counsel (and clerk) your thoughtful list of likely groups of documents, once you have finished your review of what the Team has saved from your own ESI.

Rule 26(g) also contains the aptly-named "stop and think" requirement—litigation counsel must make a reasonable inquiry to the client before handing over "evidence." By signing, the lawyer swears under oath that, after inquiry, what is being delivered is all there is. Use this to your advantage, and make sure the forensics/IT side of your Team is ready not only to make the detailed procedures affidavit, but also ready to testify, in detail, about exactly what the ESI search strategy was and what the collection protocol was, confirming that the discovery response is the whole truth about your evidence.

An employee giving the deer-in-the-headlights look in an oral deposition under oath about how ESI was collected and analyzed, or worse, giving the judge and jury that look, will not be anyone's best moment. An inaccurate affidavit supported by inaccurate and incomplete testimony about a sloppy search of ESI is a strong signal to the judge that there are also other sloppy evidence practices going on.

Parenthetically, you, after being careful to document your Team's preservation strategy and subsequent orderly analysis of ESI, may find this idea useful in pursuing any lack of detailed forensic documentation by the other side.

Your own internal use of well-developed search terms with a reliable search tool will get you through the preliminary gathering/sorting phase. Here is the chance for you to simplify later ESI exchanges, by having your list of ESI search terms for document sorting already prepared. When the lawsuit is filed and you come to the Rule 26(f) "first contact" meet-and-confer with the other side, your entire Team will be ready to be supremely cooperative, as commanded by the Rule.

You can then cheerfully point out to the court the many ways in which the other side is failing to comply with the cooperation and proportionality requirements of amended Rule 1 as well as Rules 26 and 34, and would the court consider shifting the cost of their unreasonable discovery requests to the other side? Nothing, in our experience, focuses the minds of abusive litigators like the prospect of telling their client it has to pay for your forensic expert's detailed analysis of their discovery requests, to say nothing of the forensic analysis of their preservation and analysis process.

The results of the preliminary hold will also give you the critical opportunity to find out the whole truth before you advise management about how to handle the legal situation. The Team's lawyer members can't shape a reliable narrative for the litigation or settlement negotiations, or even decide which one to go for, if you don't know all the facts.

So, get all the facts, and quit holding unnecessary ESI as soon as you are reasonably (remember proportionality?) certain you have all the facts, both good and bad. If you know the bad news early, the risk management member of the Team can help you advise upper management about settlement issues before the price goes up.

Then, of course, the Team members can congratulate themselves on a great job done in record time, and get back to their regular jobs.

THE "OTHER" HOLD NOTICE—WHEN YOU INTEND TO SUE SOMEONE

We've been talking about the in-house hold notice—the one required by the Rules, which alerts your own organization to preserve ESI. Here is a brief consideration of the "other" hold notice, often referred to as the "ESI preservation letter." This is the communication from your lawyers to the person or organization that will be your organization's target in a future lawsuit.

The ESI preservation letter has many of the same elements as the in-house hold notice. Its primary function is to alert the likely defendant that you are aware of a triggering event, requesting that the defendant-to-be also do whatever is necessary to preserve their own digital evidence. You obviously need the date(s), location(s), any key players on their side that you know of (whether by name or by job title), and any other information about the triggering event by which a reasonable person could identify the ESI that should be preserved.

For all the obvious reasons, faster is better with the ESI preservation letter. The longer you wait while attempting to be perfect, the more digital information disappears into the other organization's auto-delete. It is preferable to send a preliminary heads'-up preservation letter, indicating that further details will follow if necessary to clarify the scope of the needed preservation on their part.

The preservation letter to a potential target is not part of your own preservation obligation under the Rules. You may use this tool or not, depending on your view of the target's likelihood of instituting a hold without your alert about what you view as a triggering event. This is purely a function of your possible prior experience with this person or organization, and your opinion of their legal savvy. Remember the *Pension Committee* case we discussed in Chapter 2—where groups of extremely savvy investors knew they were going to sue, yet failed to preserve their own evidence (and, we note, their own lawyers failed to give them the critical hold notice).

Your Team members may have useful information on this point of strategy. Your conclusion may be that you don't want to point out the triggering event for various tactical reasons. Just so you know this tool is available, and don't confuse it with the real litigation hold notice that has to be sent to your own side.

AFTER THE HOLD, THE LONG VIEW OF ESI ANALYSIS

Large jumbles of ESI are not the object of the exercise. But that is what you have at this moment. Now what? Now the legal and tech Team members are tested on their fluency in each other's languages.

The ESI needs to be sorted to identify the evidence (think, legal terms) through technology-assisted review, such as predictive coding and machine learning (think, tech terms).

The carefully considered and well-drafted hold notice will give the legal members of the Team a boost in focusing on appropriate search terms for the technology-assisted review. The forensic consultant will be familiar with current search software suitable for this task. (No worries, there are many great products available, and they are getting more and more lawyer-friendly.)

Here's a quick overview of technology-assisted review. It is a highly-structured method of teaching a complex software program to bring you what you want out of many thousands of documents (machine learning). In each iteration of the search, the search vocabulary is refined to bring fewer useless documents and more useful documents. The process of refining the search terms and parameters is often called predictive coding.

That three-sentence summary is obviously extremely simplistic, since many of the software programs take as many as thirty steps just to get to the first run at the universe of ESI to be searched. It is not for amateurs, but a reasonably experienced litigator with coaching from a reasonably articulate forensic consultant can learn the process.

We have said that it is like training a puppy to bring back only the stick you threw—an analogy that has predictably offended several tech consultants. The basic offense? Their software is clearly smarter than any puppy. We agree. The process remains iterative, however—many many many carefully structured repetitions of the same action, each one more focused, until very few unwanted sticks are dropped at your feet. But make no mistake, from the perspective of proportionality and reasonableness, technology-assisted review is recognized by the courts as an appropriate way to find evidence among thousands of documents.

It is useful for you to have developed your review procedure ahead of the Rule 26(f) meet-and-confer, so your Team will be ready to exchange search methodologies with your opponent's team, as we will discuss in detail in Chapter 11.

The Rule 26 Meet-and-Confer—Your Best Chance to Control the ESI Exchange

NEWLY AMENDED RULE 26 MEANS WHAT IT SAYS

The judicial drafters of the 2015 Rules amendments intended, among other things, to put an end to ESI gamesmanship, and to firmly entrench the concepts of proportionality and cooperation in the evidence discovery process. Strengthening the electronic evidence process in Rule 26 is among the major elements of the amendments.

The Lawsuit Has Been Filed—Now Where Are We?

At this very early point in the litigation, the Complaint (stating generally the plaintiff's claims against the defendant) has been filed with the court and is in the hands of the defendant. The defendant's pre-Answer preliminary motions (wrong party, wrong court, too late, etc.) may not yet have been disposed of, and the defendant's Answer may or may not be on file, along with any counterclaims by the defendant against the plaintiff. Despite much preliminary maneuvering yet to come, the battle lines have been drawn.

Amended Rule 16 has shortened the time before the initial scheduling conference (which is actually a hearing before the judge, but without evidence or witnesses). Before that conference, Rule 26(f) requires the plaintiff and defendant, through their lawyers, to meet.

Now the lawyers, backed up by their teams (or not), get down to the work of setting terms for exchanging evidence, including electronic evidence.

As the case begins, the trial lawyers and in-house counsel might like to know what the person in the black robe is thinking on the subject of electronic evidence. That is easy to find out in the federal court system. The Federal Judicial Center (the training center for federal judges) has updated its "Benchbook for Federal District Judges." The Benchbook is the judge's detailed set of guidelines for every possible aspect of case management (both civil and criminal). You can read the ESI sections of it for yourself at the Center's website.

CONTENTS

Even better, the Center has produced a second edition of "Managing Discovery of Electronic Information: A Pocket Guide for Judges." It's a 48-page summary of what the judge expects you to already be up to speed on. Feel free to download it. Then share it and discuss it. The entire Team should know in general what it says.

ANOTHER BRIEF TOUR THROUGH THE AMENDED RULES

Here are the critical numbers, from the ESI perspective, as of December 1, 2015: 1, 16, 26, 34 and 37.

Lawyer members of the Team should have copies of the 2015 Rules amendments, with the associated committee notes, at hand. The "Summary of the Report of the Judicial Conference Committee on Rules of Practice and Procedure" (September 2014 Judicial Conference meeting, Agenda E-19, at the Judicial Conference's website) is an excellent guide to the overall goals of various groups of amendments.

Other Team members, this is your chance to understand what the ESI amendments are supposed to accomplish in the actual world of trial preparation, so that you know you were facing in the right direction when you went into "hold" mode when the triggering event happened.

Amended Rule 1 now prominently features the requirements for proportionality (that the cost to resolve the dispute should not even approach the amount that is in dispute) and cooperation (that "zealous advocacy" is not the same as "litigate them into the ground" aggression).

Amended Rule 16 features changes to case management, especially subjects for the initial scheduling order, to move the case along more quickly in the early stage. Notably, the scheduling order can specifically address ESI preservation and production. These are linked to Federal Rule of Evidence 502 (protecting privileged and confidential information). These changes are supposed to curtail excessive expense in ESI production, among other things.

The first steps in discovery are dictated by Rule 26. Rule 26(a)(1) requires each side to promptly identify its key players, and to actually provide to the other side copies or identification of relevant documents (including ESI) and physical items of evidence.

This ties in with Rules 16 and 26(f), the requirements for the parties to confer at least 21 days before the first scheduling conference with the judge. The parties must have a joint plan for discovery ready for the judge to consider at the scheduling conference. The plan will be adopted by the court as a scheduling order, which will direct the parties' activities in evidence discovery up to the trial date.

Notably, the 2015 Amendments to Rules 16 and 26(f) now provide that preservation and production of ESI are proper subjects to include in the scheduling order. As a result of that, the parties must necessarily discuss ESI preservation at the Rule 26(f) meet-and-confer, so that the issue of preservation is raised and disposed of by the parties and by the court.

In most cases this process is facilitated by the forensic consultant on the Team (often referred to in Rule 26 discussions as the "e-discovery liaison"), who should have experience in negotiating the technical details of Rule 26(f) agreements for the production of electronic data. For practical reasons, the consultant must be accompanied by a knowledgeable representative from the IT department, to assist in resolving logistics and scheduling issues.

Both of these technical advisors must understand from the outset that amended Rules 26 and 34(b)(2)(B) require your Team's lawyers to "produce" (hand over) your relevant ESI or to allow the opponent (presumably through their own technical experts) to "inspect, copy, test, or sample" your digital evidence where it is kept. This would be the storage servers to which it has been moved under the litigation hold right after the triggering event. The opponent's lawyers must, preliminarily, make a written request describing the types of information they want to look at. Rule 34(b)(1)(A) requires that the request be specific as to the "item or category of items" they wish to inspect.

When the Rule 34 production/inspection is done after the Rule 26(f) meet-and-confer, it should (theoretically) go off without a hitch, because of the specifics negotiated at the meet-and-confer and included in the scheduling order.

However, a new addition to Rule 26(d)(2) allows a party to send a Rule 34 request for production and inspection of documents (including ESI) to the opponent **before** the Rule 26(f) meeting. There appears to be a general expectation by the amendment drafters that those "early" production requests may be subjects for negotiation at the meet-and-confer, given the general likelihood that those preliminary requests may be inappropriately broad or vague.

We have not attempted here to exhaustively analyze the 2015 Rules amendments. There are lots of seminars available to do that for you, sometimes in startling detail. Please take advantage of them, whether you are a seasoned courtroom warrior looking for an update, or in-house counsel who couldn't think of a huge enough amount to get you to sit at the counsel table during your client's trial, though you're still in need of litigation management strategies.

STAY FOCUSED ON THE E-DISCOVERY GOALS

The key e-discovery goals for both inside and outside counsel in the meet-and-confer negotiation process under Rule 26(f) are first, to obtain agreement to an ESI strategy which limits the amount of material to be searched and/or produced, and second, to control the cost of evidence production (including ESI) at a reasonable level consistent with the complexity of the issues and the opposing party's requests. This is simply the direct application of the new Rule 1 requirement of proportionality, through your Team's technical side personnel.

It is a counter-productive strategy for any litigator to state as a preliminary negotiation gambit that there is no electronic evidence. It is not believable in this day and age that such a situation exists in a functioning business. Even in cases where the facts are all related to physical evidence, there is always some amount of supporting electronic evidence that should shed light on the other facts of the case. For example, location data from a cell phone can establish its user's location at a particular time (and whether the phone was in use at that moment). In the same way, the internal electronics in a vehicle or machine are almost never irrelevant.

Keep Calm—The Seventh Circuit E-Discovery Pilot Program Has the Answers

Just as the Sedona Conference and the International Organization for Standardization (ISO) have already thought long and hard in print about the ESI preservation-to-production process in general, so a pilot project by the federal trial courts of the Seventh Circuit (upper Midwest) has gone nationwide with its focused thinking about ESI during discovery under the Rules. The project is therefore specific to American litigation practice. It is called, predictably, the Seventh Circuit Electronic Discovery Pilot Program.

The three Principles developed by the Pilot Program during its development phases from 2009 to 2015 have spread not only across the United States but into international litigation practice. That diversity of interest across many jurisdictions indicates that the entire Team could benefit from a moment or two studying the Principles:

(1)   General Principles—Purpose, Cooperation, and Discovery Proportionality;

(2)   Early Case Assessment Principles—Duty to Meet and Confer on Discovery and to Identify Disputes for Early Resolution, E-Discovery Liaison(s), Preservation Requests and Orders, Scope of Preservation, Identification of ESI, Production Format; and

(3)   Education Principles—Judicial Expectations of Counsel, and Duty of Continuing Education.

The five pages of Principles are not just generalities and wishful thinking about make-nice in e-discovery. They are specific, practical steps for obtaining cooperation and proportionality in ESI discovery, and what to do if you can't get those from your opponent.

The Principles prominently feature use of your Team's forensic consultant as your "liaison" in creating a technically useful scheduling order through the Rule 26(f) meet-and-confer.

THE TEAM'S PRE-MEETING STRATEGY SESSION

From your Team's perspective, the Rule 26(f) meeting with the other side's lawyers and (we hope) ESI liaison is a matter for serious pre-meeting strategizing. The pre-meeting strategy session is the moment you bring together the Team's knowledge of the facts that are in dispute, and the ESI you have identified and preserved, including where and how to find it post-preservation.

Your forensic consultant reappears for this strategy session. The "Meeting Team" must have, at the end of the strategy session, an updated and in-depth knowledge of your organization's systems and devices, suitable for presentation to the other side's lawyers and technical team. (We are assuming their lawyers will also bring their forensic liaison and tech team to the meet-and-confer—their problem, not yours.)

The pre-meeting strategy session will have three parts, which need to be melded into a discovery strategy: (1) IT's detailed information about devices, systems, and technical details of your preservation processes; (2) in-house counsel's contributions to the overall legal strategy—systems functions plus management structures from the business operations perspective; and (3) litigation counsel's strategy for defining the legal facts through appropriate evidence.

If you haven't done so already (depending on the development of the case as the lawyers prepare the Complaint or Answer), you need to gather the technical details of the collection process and the lawyers' initial collection strategies from the triggering event and litigation hold notice. These belong in an affidavit by the individual who supervised the hold process, including both collection and preservation, showing precisely how the ESI hold requirements have been met. It will be accurate, orderly, and in-depth. It will also be ready for you to compare to whatever the other side has to say on the subject of their own litigation hold process.

In this way, the Team is ready with a strategy to meet the fundamental purpose of discovery, which is to find and analyze all reliable evidence for each element of the legal case, from your own side as well as the opponent's side.

Obviously the Team leader for the meet-and-confer is your litigation counsel (your meet-and-confer "first chair," if you have more than one trial lawyer on the Team). Before going into the meet-and-confer, litigation counsel needs to know what is available to offer, plus what to ask for. Your Team is ready. You just need to get the information organized in a way that is useful to litigation counsel.

THE MEET-AND-CONFER: A STRATEGIC OVERVIEW

The knowledge your Team brings together will include the identities of all your key players, plus specifics of the ESI that has been preserved from each key player, and from all systems and devices, and the technical method of preservation and analysis. The technical information gives your Meeting Team the ability to intelligently discuss the technical issues for the other side's inspection of your preserved ESI and how it came to be preserved.

Your Meeting Team, naturally, will expect the same level of technical information from the other side, so that you can propose an appropriate electronic search strategy to identify evidence in their preserved ESI. And of course, you will also have a strategy already at hand at the meet-and-confer if the other side has neglected its duty to preserve its own ESI.

What to Offer

Litigation counsel, as the Meeting Team leader, needs to be able to articulate the scope of all your preserved ESI, some of which will be evidence, and some of which will turn out to be just peripheral or background information (perhaps useful for understanding the nature of the dispute, but not proof of an element of the case).

This means, in effect, being ready to offer in an orderly way all ESI collected under the supervision of your forensic consultant by your IT Team members. You will need to include technical information about the devices and system elements from which collection was made, the technical details of the collection process, and the technical details of the devices to which the ESI was transferred for preservation.

Just a reminder—the lawyers can ask each other for documents and ESI information that will be useful in identifying evidence, even if that information is not itself evidence. This is why your Team needed to think broadly back at the time of the triggering event and litigation hold notice.

As You Offer, You Also Ask

The key to this part of the meet-and-confer (besides having the Team's forensic/IT strategy already in hand) is for litigation counsel to know what not to accept. In order for your Team to do a complete and efficient job of collecting and evaluating the other side's ESI (thereby having the raw material for identifying the actual evidence), you need the same things you have just offered—detailed descriptions of all devices containing ESI, including original devices and storage devices, and including the technical details of all ESI transfers and handling during their collection and preservation process—all of this for each of their key players.

Accept No Excuses

One of your early questions to the other side is the date on which they did their litigation hold and preservation after the triggering event. Everyone on your meet-and-confer Team needs to know, for different reasons, when the other side's preservation happened compared to yours. A second question will be precisely how they did it.

This is a hard-ball moment for your litigation counsel, backed up by the Team. Accept no excuses, no weaseling, about inadequacies your Team recognizes in the opponent's ESI preservation process, most particularly about improper handling of ESI by forensically-untrained support staff (including "IT" personnel without appropriate certifications) and unsupervised collection and preservation "techniques" that have no basis in good forensics. Do not let notions about courtesy get in the way of a proper ESI discovery plan. The answer to attempted intimidation is always, "Please answer the question: what techniques by what personnel?"

It is not inappropriate or unprofessional to require the other side to hand over affidavits from the individuals who did their collection, describing the exact credentials of the individuals who directed and carried out their ESI collection and preservation, plus technical details of what they collected, why they collected and preserved only that ESI, and why their collection and preservation methods were forensically proper. These affidavits are often the basis for later testimony by "business records custodians" and related cross-examination. You will, of course, have your custodian's affidavit ready to hand over if the other side asks.

Don't worry about the judge thinking you're over the line with these requests for technical information and documentation of the process at this stage, assuming you have been reasonably courteous in asking for them. Reread the ESI training manuals from the Federal Judicial Center, and (of course) the amended Rules.

Use Your Technical Knowledge to Support Your Legal Negotiations

The Team has spent serious time and effort in all phases of the ESI preservation and analysis. You have already identified, preserved, processed, reviewed, and analyzed the data collected as a result of the litigation hold. You have applied appropriate technology-assisted review and predictive coding techniques to the ESI. You know what is there to be found, so you could advise management about the appropriate risk management analysis elements. This is the moment to bring it all to the table.

The knowledge your Meeting Team brings includes specifics of the ESI that has been preserved from all systems and devices, and the technical method of preservation. The technical information gives your Meeting Team the ability to intelligently discuss the technical issues for the other side's inspection of your preserved ESI and how it came to be preserved. You are not doing this to be "the bad guys" at the table. You are doing it to comply with the amended Rules, and to get your pretrial discovery, including e-discovery, done promptly and efficiently.

Your Meeting Team, naturally, should expect the same level of technical information from the other side, so that the two sides can jointly propose an appropriate electronic search strategy, to identify all sources of evidence in the preserved ESI.

And of course, you will also have a strategy ready at the meet-and-confer if the other side has neglected its duty to preserve its own ESI at the time of the triggering event.

The amended Rules provide for the possibility of a multi-part, phased meeting. Take advantage of this opportunity. Do not be rushed into accepting inferior discovery terms.

No Delivery of ESI Content Without Metadata— When Paper is Not an Option

If the other side offers to give you printed copies of their electronically generated documents, on the pretext that paper is easier for you to review, the answer (politely) is "No", unless you are requesting information which necessarily is not machine searchable.

Your Team members know the answer. Obviously, for documents for which the metadata is reasonably likely to be irrelevant, printed copies may be perfectly acceptable, and your cooperation is required in order to make that distinction.

You may need to know the creation and revision history of some kinds of ESI, not least of all because you need to know if you have the "latest and greatest" version of critical documents, and that what you have are complete documents. If the electronic document has been edited by someone other than the originating author, you want to know. This applies to certain kinds of email exchanges as well as "documents" and data-base information. The Team should have identified these in the strategy session.

In connection with discussing the metadata issue, both at the strategy session and at the meet-and-confer, remember to check the local rules of the court you are assigned to. More and more courts are requiring specific designations in the scheduling order about the scope of metadata in e-discovery.

Know the answer in advance—do you only want system file metadata (the history of a particular document along with its current contents), or substantive application metadata (showing all changes made to every successive version of the document)?

Note that the second kind of metadata can expose privileged or confidential information, which must be addressed by special agreements limiting production. The special agreements should include "claw-back" provisions. These provisions ensure that any privileged or confidential information obtained during e-discovery must be returned to the control of the producing party and cannot be used for any purpose, either in the litigation or elsewhere.

Going Native, or Not

"Native format" just means the electronic format in which a particular electronic item was created and maintained within its original system or device. This is usually the most convenient way for documents to be maintained and stored within the organization. In general, you want ESI delivered in native format, as you have stored ESI after the hold notice.

If the other side requests ESI in non-native format, you are entitled to an explanation showing why non-native format is reasonable. Your Team members are ready to spot a pretext when they hear one.

If your organization uses specialized and/or proprietary software, as is often the case with complex databases, you will need to cooperate in developing a work-around. Your forensic liaison and IT Team members at the meet-and-confer will need to have a "tech-speak" moment with the opposing liaison, to figure out a way for the other side to get the information it reasonably requests without going through an access nightmare. Merely for example, can information in a complex database be obtained by an agreed-upon set of queries to the database?

You, naturally, are already prepared to respond to the same issue from the other side if they have proprietary software and/or database complexities. It is yet another demonstration of cooperation and proportionality to have your answer at hand when the other side raises the subject. (You are keeping extensive notes of the technical as well as legal issues at the meeting, right?)

This technical two-way street can get crowded. Give yourselves and the opposing team time to work through the issues related to database information. You may well need to work out database access technical issues about your own ESI ahead of time, perhaps even before the strategy session, to be sure the other side can get information they are entitled to in a reasonably restricted and orderly way. However, this does not mean you need to let the other side waste your time stalling about technical issues.

The TIFF Trap—Don't Fall Into It

Here's an initial test of how the entire pre-trial discovery process is going to go. If the other side's litigation counsel comes to the meet-and-confer with the assumption that your side is staffed by ESI morons, you will get an offer for them to deliver all their ESI to you as TIFF files, since in their "opinion" that is most convenient for everyone. They may even tell you they customarily maintain all their preserved ESI in TIFF format. They may even tell you that with a straight face.

Everyone on the Team should know from way back that TIFF is a photo format. The ESI will be delivered as a long string of completely unsearchable blocks. The words will be formatted as if they were just dark/light portions of a photo image.

Politely, after the suppressed snickering dies down on your side, decline. Then get down to the business of defining the appropriate delivery formats, based on the technical information they will (maybe) give you. See if there is any reason not to "go native" on most delivery formats.

THE OPERATIVE WORD IS "CONFER"

We hope we haven't given the impression that you should expect the Rule 26(f) meet-and-confer and other early contacts to be negative experiences. There are certainly plenty of uncooperative and ignorant people out there. But with a professional approach, demonstrating that you intend to assist the opponent in getting e-discovery done right, you can make the amended Rules work to your advantage.

Give an uninformed opponent a gentle push in the right direction, so you get what you need without raising blood pressure on either side. Feel free to stand on the Rules with the fully informed but obnoxious opponent. Remember, the goal here is the Rule 1 "just, speedy, and inexpensive determination" of your case.

The whole point of the meet-and-confer is to exchange proposals and information. You will be prepared with all the technical as well as legal information your opponent will need to get the joint discovery plan/scheduling order drafted. The challenge is to get past the traditional elbows-out posturing, and on to the good part—exchanging as much of your technical and legal information as the other side wants for as much of their technical and legal information as you can get. Then, with your Team's legal expertise, the scheduling order drafting starts.

This is the moment for your Team members to convey to their opposite numbers on the other side the specific technical and legal requirements for adequate and efficient discovery. This is a communications challenge, just as learning each other's languages was when you originally formed the Team.

Search Terms—Think About Dispute Details, So ESI Searches Are Productive

Handing over or receiving several terabytes of data is not the object of the game. The object is for each side to find evidence that tends to show the factual universe of the dispute. Finding those facts requires focused searching, through the use of electronic searches.

"Technology-assisted review" and "predictive coding" are terms that will lead the Team deep into the field of electronic search strategies. The basic concept is that with a very-carefully considered list of terms, electronic search software can review thousands of documents and bring back the ones that are responsive to your inquiry. Obviously, creating these lists of search terms is a blend of both legal concepts (based on knowing the evidence needed to prove all the elements of the case) and technological concepts. We are not going to recommend or criticize any of the search software that is currently available. By the time this book is in your hands those suggestions will be out of date anyway. Just be aware—using it requires two separate logical approaches (and a lot of practice) to develop a working search strategy.

Developing appropriately limited search terms for ESI is one of the requirements for the meet-and-confer, so the searches can be accurately reflected in the scheduling order. The legal members of your Team must be able to inform the judge about the scope of the e-discovery process, including demonstrating that the discussions at the Rule 26(f) meet-and-confer were properly focused on the actual disputed factual issues in the litigation.

Your forensic consultant "liaison" should be ready, after the strategy session we discussed above, to join with the litigators to guide the development of appropriate e-discovery search terms, based on the dispute analysis by the Team's legal members, and based on the available software for effectively conducting such searches within the parameters of your systems and devices and the other side's systems and devices.

The joint development of search terms at the meet-and-confer is one of the cooperative elements of the meet-and-confer, as the strategy-session development of search terms is one of the teamwork elements.

Technical Oversight of E-Discovery Production

Your forensic consultant and IT Team members are there for a critical reason—so the lawyers don't have to supervise the technical aspects of e-discovery production. It is important for your forensic consultant, as your "e-discovery liaison," to be in charge of arranging the technical details of the scheduling order and the e-discovery process.

Technical supervision by your Team's forensic liaison personnel must be a requirement during your Team's ESI collection efforts from the other side, and during their collection from your stored ESI, whether or not the other side is technologically knowledgeable. If they are, they should require the same from you for their forensic liaison.

As a reminder, Rule 26(a)(1) designates the "initial disclosures" each side must immediately make to the other, including the identities of their key players and the types of discoverable information that are available.

Other than those disclosures, you only get what you specifically ask for, and only under the terms of the discovery portion of the Rules. Vague or generalized discovery requests will no longer be acceptable under the Rules, as reflected in the Rules Committee's Report and the Committee Notes associated with each amended Rule, as well as the Federal Judicial Center's "Benchbook" and the "E-Discovery Handbook for Judges."

Be certain the other side understands your position: that your Team expects focused and technically appropriate e-discovery from them, as you will deliver focused and technically appropriate e-discovery requests to them. All of this will be reflected in the discovery plan/scheduling order.

The Rules amendments did not change one fundamental aspect of ESI discovery. Under the "inspection and copying" provision of Rule 26, after the Rule 26(a) initial disclosures, you collect from their systems, and they collect from yours. This means you are entitled to examine all their devices and systems, and they are entitled to examine yours, not just the area to which ESI has been moved for preservation, but only to the extent they can demonstrate to the judge that your litigation hold was inadequate.

To the extent your Team documents in detail your collection and preservation protocols, you lessen the need for intrusions into your operating systems and devices, long after the triggering event.

That being said, there is absolutely no reason for you to allow forensically untrained representatives of the other side anywhere near your systems and devices. You need to know the forensic credentials of any individual who is going to be conducting "inspection and copying" from any of your systems and/or devices. And each such individual needs to do that inspection and copying under the observation and supervision of your forensic consultant and IT Team members, to prevent even inadvertent (meaning ignorant) actions that could damage your operations. Part of your meet-and-confer negotiations must include specific arrangements for appropriately documented representatives to access your ESI. This is not just a litigation scheduling issue, it is a business protection issue.

Each side is also entitled to all necessary access software for reviewing electronic information, regardless of the location of the ESI being produced for inspection and copying. You will be ready for that request, and you should expect the other side to be prepared to do likewise.

You will certainly want to give the technical as well as legal details of your preservation strategy to the other side, and require the same in return, if only to dispel the occasional bouts of discovery paranoia. Cooperation is the watchword under the amended Rules. Anything you ask for you should have already offered.

Obviously, with the delays caused by pre-litigation fact gathering, complaint drafting, etc., things will be very different in both sides' systems and devices by the time the meet-and-confer begins the discovery process during the lawsuit. This is the point when your detailed technical affidavits about your litigation hold and preservation process will stand you in good stead. You can show that you have properly identified and correctly saved everything that would reasonably be necessary to sort out the facts, and that you have executed a preservation strategy proportional to the dispute.

PRESERVATION ORDERS—BE QUICK, BE PRECISE

While your Team is supposed to assume that the other side has reacted to the triggering event by identifying, collecting, preserving and analyzing all of their appropriate ESI just as your Team did, we all know that... well, things happen. Or don't happen. If at the meet-and-confer you discover the lawyers and/or client representatives for the other side are technically clueless, and have no forensic liaison to make the ESI discovery process work properly under the amended Rules, your Team needs to be ready for action, again.

When your meet-and-confer Team finds out in a reliable way that the other side has compromised ESI by improper collection (including destruction or non-preservation of metadata), or that the other side has done only an unreasonably limited litigation hold and preservation, or even preserved nothing at all, you need to immediately alert the judge.

Your Team needs to prepare for at least a conference with the judge and the other side, or perhaps even a hearing to create a record of the exact extent to which ESI evidence has not been properly preserved as required by amended Rule 37(e), or has been compromised, and to get a preservation order to save what is still available.

The preservation order will require some technical expertise from your Team's forensic liaison and IT members, so that the situation is not made worse by forensic amateurs on the other side ignorantly trying to avoid sanctions by improper collection techniques.

Obviously the legal members of the Team will be contemplating their options under amended Rule 37(e) for orders by the court to work around the damage and/or to obtain appropriately limited punishments, such as cost shifting, for the spoliation. These considerations will require input from the technical side also.

THE FINAL PRODUCT OF A GOOD MEET-AND-CONFER

Finally, you have what you need—a reliable route to proportionate and orderly e-discovery. Your scheduling order, based on the Rule 26(f) report, will limit cost and false steps.

If you have gotten off on the right foot with the other side, the scheduling order will not only ease the discovery burden, it will leave room for developments as you learn more facts in discovery. "Staged discovery" means that each side starts with evidence directly addressing the obvious (in lawyer-speak, "dispositive") disputed fact issues before moving to possibly-unnecessary complexities. This is the time to suggest some preliminary agreements ("stipulations") about facts that are not (or should not be) disputed. These steps at the beginning of discovery (preferably, but not necessarily, offered for inclusion in the scheduling order) can be an excellent demonstration of your Team's focus on the requirements for cooperation and proportionality in discovery.

The first meeting with the judge, to present the proposed scheduling order at the initial scheduling conference, should not be a finger-pointing whine session. If the meet-and-confer takes more than one session, with perhaps a separate tech session, you need to put in the effort here at the front, so you have a firm grip on the process going forward under the discovery plan/scheduling order. Judges are not very receptive to violations of their orders, especially violations justified by excuses such as "I didn't know that's what they meant."

Be sure your Rule 26(f) report is clear and comprehensive about all your e-discovery issues. That way, should the other side be inspired to do something inappropriate just to run up your litigation expenses, you are ready to go straight to the judge. Failure to be both clear and comprehensive leaves you in that awkward position of agreeing by neglect to what you don't want. For example, if the other side produces documents in a format other than one you specified for a particular class of ESI, you are secure in asking the court to order double-production at their own expense. If you haven't actually specified, you may well be stuck trying to deal with a large quantity of inaccessible, unsearchable data, or having to pay for double production of that data while the pre-trial schedule is running.

Failing to specify the technical details can also excuse the other side from having to continue preserving that data, just as later failing to inspect ESI when inspection is offered can excuse their further preservation of the ESI.

Looking For A Form To Start From? A Few Resources

No one likes to be the first one to draft a new and complex form of document for the judge to sign as an order. Fortunately, the lawyers and judges of the federal Seventh Circuit trial courts have done it for you. Their website has what you need—a form scheduling order ready for you to adapt to the circumstances of your particular case and your particular systems and devices.

For that and other resources, including some of our personal favorite up-to-the-minute blogs about electronic discovery, check the Resources Appendix to this book.

CHAPTER 12

A Glance at International Issues— Never Assume!

INTERNATIONAL ISSUES IN ESI PRESERVATION AND E-DISCOVERY—A VERY BRIEF LOOK

Even the smallest companies do business internationally, courtesy of such services as the Export-Import Bank, and other lenders focused on cross-border economic development. But, as we know, things happen. Whether your international partner is a private or public entity, from the smallest deal to the mega-deal, it is smarter to be prepared than surprised.

Thinking internationally obviously requires reliable, up-to-date, unbiased information. You need to know about not only the economic structure of your international business partners, but also about their legal systems and cultural expectations. This section is about finding resources to help you make good ESI preservation decisions at the front end, before a dispute, because you may not have an opportunity to make them once the contracts are signed and the deal is in progress.

We are going to review very quickly a lot of international commercial transactions concepts, just so we're generally all on the same page when we talk about ESI and your internationalized dispute-resolution Team.

THERE IS NOT HERE—A BRIEF CONSIDERATION OF COMMON LAW AND CIVIL LAW TRADITIONS

Ready for a gross over-simplification? The world is divided into two parts.

Let's fill that out a bit. There are more than 200 independent countries and/or separate dependent territories in the world, according to the United Nations, the International Olympic Committee, and other people who keep track of such things (each of which gives us a different number). Each country has its own separate justice system, reflecting its own history, culture, business tradition, etc.

That being said, the very large majority of those legal systems fall into just two historical groups: the "common law" tradition, including the United States and other countries with historical ties to Britain; and the "civil law" tradition,

CONTENTS

145

(Continued)

CONTENTS

including the countries with historical ties to the other European powers, Russia and many Asian countries with independent legal traditions.

Grossly over-simplifying again, here are the fundamental structures and differences between the two systems.

Common Law—A Shared British Heritage of the U.S., Canada, and the Commonwealth

The common law system developed in Britain after the Norman Conquest and through the medieval period and Enlightenment, as kings consolidated political power and combined many of the justice traditions from various parts of the country. As the legal system developed, judges rather than noblemen (or politicians) settled disputes. The judge in a specific case did not apply a written legal code, but the long tradition of the courts. With a few overarching rules, such as those set out in *Magna Carta*, the Great Charter of 1215, judges followed the decisions of prior judges (especially decisions issued in higher courts through appeals) as guidance in their own decisions. Statutes (individual laws), passed by local and national political bodies, gave additional guidance and boundaries for judges. Some of those laws on the same topic were eventually gathered into Codes for ease of reference.

Within this tradition, as the legal training system developed, judges became the "referees" between two adversarial lawyers presenting their versions of the facts—the development of the concept of fact-based evidence. Also within this tradition, the jury became a central element—local citizens joining to weigh the evidence, to determine the facts, to which the judge would apply the law.

The statutes in a common law country never provide the whole answer to a dispute. The judges were (and are) on their own in sorting out disputes and determining which party will be the winner. They arrive at a judgment by applying traditional or customary local law, as it developed case by case in the local courts. Each case became part of the greater legal tradition, which was passed down orally, then by written case summaries through many generations of lawyers and judges trained in the same tradition.

The legal tradition as applied by early common law judges was also affected by canon (religious) law and maritime law, both of which were based on Roman law rather than local legal tradition. In addition, the procedures for practicing before the common law courts became highly stratified over time, leading to periods of serious systemic injustice, which had to be corrected by political action through statutes.

Statutes exist at all levels of the court systems in common law countries. But in general the judge, not the statute, is at the center of the justice systems in Great Britain, the United States, Canada, and the other present or former British colonies. As each country went its own way and developed its own local traditions in response to its own needs, the details of the received British tradition were overtaken by local common law as well as local statutes.

As a result, it would be a disaster waiting to happen if either party to an international transaction between common law countries were to assume that the other side had the same specific common law on a particular commercial issue or a point of procedure.

For this reason alone, your team needs lawyers who are knowledgeable and experienced about both jurisdictions. Never assume, even about the common law. Never assume, even about our English-speaking northern neighbor (because, among other things, it is also our French-speaking northern neighbor). There is not here.

Civil Law—The Codified Law is Comprehensive: Mexico and Other Non-British Countries

The other major part of the legal world is the civil law tradition. It is the basis for nearly all legal systems outside of the British common law tradition. The civil law tradition includes groups of countries with common languages based on a common colonial past, such as the former French, Belgian, Spanish and Portuguese colonies. It also includes countries which have never been part of those European colonial empires, such as China, Japan and Russia.

The European civil law tradition developed from the comprehensive code of law of the Roman Empire, applicable to all members of civil society, as gathered in the sixth century at the direction of Roman Emperor Justinian.

To be clear, a civil law system is not necessarily based on Roman law. It is based on the concept of a comprehensive written set of laws, covering both the substance of various areas of law (such as tax law, criminal law, administrative or government powers law, commercial/business law, etc.) and explicit rules of procedure for use in courts of all kinds. The point is to have a written answer for every possible question, every possible situation, every possible development.

In the civil law tradition, the judge's role is to lead the inquiry into the disputed matter, to develop the evidence to reflect a reasonably complete set of the facts, and then determine the appropriate section of the codified law to give the proper outcome. In the civil law, the judge is a very active participant in the development of evidence and resolution of the dispute. The function of the jury is not as highly developed, and in fact in many instances the parties will have no right to a jury.

As with the international transaction between common law countries, don't court disaster by assuming anything about commercial transactions (or any other law) or the court system in civil law countries. Even if you regularly travel to Mexico, or other countries in the Western Hemisphere, or to Asia, or Africa, or to countries of the former Soviet Union, never assume. Even if you believe yourself to be fluent in the language and culture of the other country, make full use of the cross-border legal and forensic talent on your International Team, because there is not here.

Remember, in only a few paragraphs of summary we are more likely to leave out than include something you will later find important. Interested in dipping a little bit deeper in the distinction between common law and civil law traditions? We have some resources for you in the Resources Appendix.

CROSS-BORDER TRANSACTIONS IN GENERAL—SOME STRUCTURAL CONSIDERATIONS

If you're a lawyer, this will be a quick refresher on structural issues in cross-border commercial transactions. If you're not a lawyer, here's a quick introduction.

Contracts within the United States are made when the parties agree on the fundamental terms for a deal—who is providing what and how much it will cost. Pretty much everything else in the deal can be filled in or assumed from the type of industry the parties are in, that is, what is commercially reasonable in a transaction of this type. So, a "contract" can be written on a bar napkin, or even be a completely oral "handshake" deal, as long as both sides agree on those basic terms. This is because of the highly developed law of commercial transactions in the U.S. plus the common law of what information, in addition to "what" and "how much" makes a reasonable contract.

This is, obviously, a profoundly bad template for an international transaction, especially if the deal goes bad. But you get the idea—a contract is an agreement to exchange something of value (typically, money) for something else the parties agree is of reasonably equivalent value.

As an aside, in common law jurisdictions, by long tradition only contracts involving real estate (such as land sales and mortgages) were absolutely required to be in writing, and signed by at least the seller—a long story. Many statutes and regulations have added other types of deals to that list. But it reminds you to keep an eye on the historical issues in cross-border deals.

Once you introduce an international boundary (that is, two separate legal systems) into the equation, things quickly fall into two categories of negotiations. For nearly all routine international transactions, there are completely standard forms which have been in use for many decades. Transactions which are unusual in some way (such as exporting high tech or importing live animals) are separately negotiated down to the minutest detail, because they are generally regulated down to the minutest detail by local or national authorities on at least one side.

The routine deals are generally done with forms dictated by such international commercial groups as the International Chamber of Commerce (ICC, based in Paris). The non-routine ones require serious expertise in regulatory issues as well as commercial issues in each country (and, occasionally, maritime expertise). You can get most of that information from the ICC. Check our Resources Appendix.

A National Government or Its Agency May Be Your International Partner

When your company contracts for participation in a project located in another country (whether you provide goods or services), you may well find an agency of the host country as one of your contracting partners (perhaps even an unnamed partner)—an arrangement referred to by the World Bank as public-private partnerships ("PPPs"), which are often called "concession arrangements."

Consider the partner country's legal tradition at this point—is it in the common law or civil law tradition? The World Bank has some advice for companies that participate in PPP projects. Among those we find particularly useful is the suggestion to review not only the contract but also the country's administrative law and other laws which may apply to concession projects. Particularly in civil law countries, major contract terms are not in the contract. They are in the administrative law or even the constitution, such as rights for the government to modify or even cancel your contract, or to compel you to complete the contract even when the local conditions have altered substantially. These are based on the legal theory that the project is a public service, which is not subject to interruption. The World Bank's presentation specifically mentions the possibility that the contracting partner, your company, may be compelled to invest in advanced or upgraded technology not contemplated in the original contract. We pause to contemplate the issue of e-discovery technology in this context.

The Resource Appendix has directions to this information from the World Bank.

Cross-Border Dispute Resolution: It's In The Contract, Maybe

In many industries, and in many countries' legal systems, there are not only the stated terms on the form contract. There are also "implied" terms, which have taken on the force of contact terms as an unspoken part of the industries' and countries' commercial development. "We have always done it this way" can be a contract term, whether outsiders know about "it" or not. That includes dispute resolution terms. That also includes what will or will not be acceptable as evidence.

Naturally, dispute resolution provisions are pretty standard in international commercial contracts. They provide for the kind of resolution the parties will use if things go bad—international arbitration under a specific set of arbitration rules; litigation in some court, somewhere; or a combination of elements. It is also routine for the standard international contracts to state what country's commercial laws will be applied. It would not be unusual for an American private company doing business with a Moroccan private company to use a standard ICC form contract providing that all disputes will be resolved by arbitration, and will be held in Paris (choice of forum or venue provision), applying British commercial law (choice of laws provision). Laws of the major industrial countries are generally used in such contracts, since those countries have well-developed commercial laws. The forum for arbitration (as opposed to a trial court) might well be any large city outside the home countries of the two contracting businesses.

From our perspective, whichever form of dispute resolution you end up with (and whether you chose it or had it imposed by the other side), and whatever commercial law will be applied, the evidence preservation issues are the same. You still need to preserve, analyze and produce your electronic evidence along with other (physical and paper evidence) at least internally, in order for management to make fact-based decisions about resolving the dispute, and so the legal members of the Team can prepare efficiently to resolve the dispute.

Note that in international transactions the dispute resolution procedure is set in stone at the very beginning, in the standardized form contract. Your ability to negotiate an advantageous dispute resolution strategy ends there.

Discovery in International Arbitration

Arbitration is an alternative to trial courts, and uses one or several experts in the parties' industry instead of a judge to determine who wins and who loses. Like a trial, arbitration is an all-or-nothing approach—there is no compromise or middle ground. You win or you lose.

In international arbitration, "evidence" in the sense of documents which meet the standards of proof set out in one party's judicial procedures, is very limited. Discovery in the sense it is practiced in American courts is usually not allowed. Defensible forensic practices may not be possible in collecting what little ESI you may be allowed to collect from your opponent. Know the details up-front.

Nevertheless, you should be prepared for a reasonable approximation of the litigation hold, if for no other purpose than to advise your own management of the issues for negotiation or for presentation to an arbitrator about the conduct of the project.

Discovery in International Mediation

It is possible, though not routine, to provide for mediation as a preliminary step in dispute resolution. Mediation provides for an independent third party to attempt to find a compromise, by negotiating a settlement between the parties. It is not a win/lose resolution but a give-and-take, in which each party gives up some of what it would be entitled to in a trial or arbitration. This approach is useful if a project is in progress, and both sides have some motivation to get past the dispute and finish the project.

From the evidence perspective, please note that unlike trial or arbitration processes, mediation is not particularly about "the facts." It is about re-establishing trust or at least communication between the parties, in an attempt to get a contract or project back up out of the ditch and on the road again. In general, opportunities for discovery will be limited or even non-existent in the mediation process. That being said, a limited version of the litigation hold is wise, in case the mediation fails and you find yourselves facing arbitration or trial.

Before the Contract Decisions, the Team Analyzes the Dispute Resolution Issues

Your entire International Team can contribute to the discussion if some Team members aren't already familiar with every one of the stated and implied terms of the dispute resolution provision in the cross-border contract, including the ability to deal with ESI preservation and cross-border production.

DATA-RELATED CROSS-BORDER ISSUES: PERSONAL DATA PRIVACY LAWS ARE SERIOUS

One of the critical limits on cross-border evidence exchanges is the data privacy issue. In some countries, data privacy has become a hot-button political issue. Improper disclosure or transfer of personal data is a jailable offense in some countries. The International Team needs to know the details of data privacy and protection in any country or region where you intend to do business, completely aside from any commercial issues about dispute resolution.

When any company's data must cross international borders, unique problems arise. This is particularly so in the collection and transportation of ESI to be used as evidence. Evidence is intended to be made public, to at least everyone who sees it on your own side, plus everyone who sees it on the other side, plus the judge and all the courtroom personnel, plus the jury. Plus perhaps, the media in a small or large way. And when papers are filed electronically containing information summarizing evidence in support of a particular position, as it generally is in the U.S. federal courts and most state courts, everyone in the world who can get to a computer gets a look. That's not much privacy.

An Extremely Brief Survey of Some Countries' Data Privacy Laws

At least 114 countries have specific privacy laws or regulations restricting the movement of personally identifiable information. Unfortunately there is little uniformity in how that information is defined. In fact, even within the United States there is great diversity (and therefore confusion) in handling data related to individuals. Only three states have no privacy laws as of mid-2015, and rely completely on the federal privacy laws.

America's two closest neighbors, Canada and Mexico, have strict regulation and serious punishments for improper movement of any data that comes within their separate definitions of "private."

Canada

Canada has a Privacy Commissioner, as do many other countries. That federal office is tasked with both interpreting and enforcing data-privacy laws, involving personal information handled by federal government agencies (the Privacy Act) as well as personal information handled by commercial businesses (the Personal Information Protection and Electronic Documents Act, or PIPEDA).

We note a warning on the Canadian Privacy Commissioner's website, directed specifically to lawyers. It points out that taking a laptop or portable data device out of the country may violate the privacy regulations, since the contents of such devices are subject to detailed inspection at customs checkpoints. This is not just addressed to Canadian lawyers, but to other lawyers entering Canada and taking ESI back across the border.

The Office of the Privacy Commissioner's website contains, in the OPC Guidance Documents area, a document titled "PIPEDA and Your Practice: A Privacy Handbook for Lawyers" which in the "International Issues" section gives an excellent tour of the complexities of handling data which may include personal information.

The Handbook contains a link to another source of reliable information about data movement best practices, the Canadian Bar Association publication, "How to Secure Your Laptop Before Crossing the Border."

The website also contains a comprehensive publication entitled "Privacy Toolkit: A Guide for Businesses and Organizations—Canada's PIPEDA."

The OPC and CBA documents are predictably polite and helpful. However, if you think the polite tone indicates Canada isn't really serious about data privacy, please note that enforcement is not just by OPC administrative action. The privacy laws are also enforced by the federal courts, which can authorize investigations by the Royal Canadian Mounted Police, with whom you should never wish to tangle.

Check our Resources Appendix.

Mexico

All of Mexico's official information about its 2010 data privacy law, the Federal Law on the Protection of Personal Data Held by Private Parties, is, naturally, in Spanish. There are however a number of reliable English-language blogsites which follow data privacy developments, including the developing Mexican data protection law and its associated regulations.

Of particular note, from our perspective, is that the Mexican law reflects the concept of *"habeas data."* Under this concept, the individual to whom personal data relates is the data owner, with the legal right to control use of the data. This ownership/control concept is not (at the moment) contained in the privacy laws and regulations of Canada or the countries of the European Union.

The Mexican equivalent of the Canadian Office of the Privacy Commissioner is the IFAI (in English, the Institute for Access to Information and Data Protection). The IFAI provides interpretive guidance as well as supervision of the regulations under the law. The Institute conducts compliance inspections and can issue monetary penalties for violations.

The Mexican privacy law does provide a specific exception to the data transfer restrictions for transfer of personal data necessary to exercise a judicial claim or defense. However, it appears that in the context of cross-border data transfers related to legal disputes the regulations are not as straightforward as that statement would appear.

Check our Resources Appendix.

The European Union and its Member Countries

The European Union is a group of independent countries, each of which has its own legal system. However, all the member countries are also subject to two levels of EU-wide regulation. The lower level of laws provides for mechanisms to "harmonize" most laws, so that goods and services (and individuals) are only minimally hindered in moving among the member countries, while allowing each country to govern itself and observe its own cultural approach to life. In some important areas, however, the EU Parliament and Commission pass and enforce specific laws that are applicable as written regardless of location in the EU.

At the moment, each EU country has its own data privacy laws. The European Union countries are also subject to the twenty-year-old, EU-wide Directive 95/46/EC, and the new General Data Protection Regulation (GDPR). The GDPR is designed to "harmonize" the data privacy policies of the member countries, so that data can flow more easily throughout the EU, while protecting data flowing out of the EU. The 1995 Directive has detailed rules on what types of information can be transported outside the EU and for what reasons.

We note in particular the EU concept of "Binding Corporate Rules" (BCR) that multinational corporations can use to demonstrate corporate attention to the concept of personal data privacy in business dealings into and out of the EU, especially out of the EU to countries that do not have personal data protection at the same level as the EU policies. BCRs are internally enforceable, effective rules of conduct for the business, which are sufficiently specific to show that the company has safeguards in place to protect personal information in the company's data transfer procedures, and that the safeguards are at least as stringent as Directive 95/46/CE. Once the BCR is approved by the National Data Protection Commissioners of the company's EU headquarters country, further external enforcement by the EU authorities is unnecessary.

That being said, a "safe harbour" provision dating from 2000 allowed data to flow between the EU and the U.S. That provision was rejected in October, 2015 by the European Court of Justice (ECJ—the EU's highest court). The basis for the ECJ's ruling was that the European Commission (the EU's administrative bureaucracy) inaccurately determined in 2000 that personal data sent to the U.S. would be suitably protected under U.S. law. The case involved the Irish subsidiary of Facebook, which transferred to the U.S. various personal information posted by an Austrian citizen. The ECJ determined that U.S. law allows the National Security Agency (and perhaps other agencies) to, in essence, violate the U.S.'s own and other countries privacy laws in the name of U.S. national security, public interest and law enforcement. The basis for the ruling was the revelations by NSA ex-contractor Edward Snowden of NSA inspection of "private" information contained in electronic communications. News media sources in the EU estimated that more than 4,400 web-based enterprises would be directly and immediately affected by the data transfer safe-harbour rule rejection.

Our Resources Appendix contains a link to the EU Justice Commission, containing specific procedural information for this business tool going forward.

China

As you know if you pay attention to international business news, China has a very strict grip on movement of data of all kinds within as well as out of China. The restrictions are not just on private or personal data, and not just on social media. The Chinese data restrictions include any business information that, from time to time, might be considered "state secret" information. The "secret" information may include information that previously appeared in publicly-accessible publications. The punishments for publishing or transferring restricted information are draconian. Stay informed, even from day to day.

We have not seen any reliable recent information in English about specific Chinese data protection laws and regulations. However, several international law firms with offices in Hong Kong and Shanghai have active news bulletin services on their websites. See our Resources Appendix as well as the major international news services.

Japan

Japanese data transfer laws and regulations are general in nature and rely on self-regulation by businesses operating in Japan. The primary general law is the Act on Protection of Personal Information (APPI), which applies to businesses that hold personal information of 5,000 or more individuals. It requires businesses to specify their uses of personal data, and to disclose to individuals the specific personal information of that individual in their files and the way that information will be used. There are similar laws applicable to personal data held by government agencies, as well as the Basic Policy, which implements the laws. Japan does not have a data-protection agency with enforcement powers similar to the Canadian Privacy Commissioner and other national privacy commissions. We have some links at the Resources Appendix.

India and other Asian Nations

India, the other populous Asian nation, also has data privacy regulations, as do commercial hubs Hong Kong, Singapore, South Korea and Taiwan. These privacy regulations are entwined with electronic discovery restrictions, reflecting the fact that most of the Asian countries are civil-law rather than common-law legal traditions, and thus have much more restricted evidence discovery procedures. Yes, the Resources Appendix.

You Get the Idea—Ask First

We have obviously neglected large areas of the world. By the time you read this, some of the information above will be out-dated. The take-away is this: data privacy and data protection are fast-growing and powerful concepts around the world. In the absence of reliable English-language information, assume data privacy restrictions are in effect. Your in-country legal consultant will be able to find the most up-to-date regulatory information, and can keep you posted about current and developing issues.

Addressing Problems with the American Approach to Evidence

Many U.S. courts have required the production of evidence from servers outside the territorial limits of the U.S., which has predictably irritated or even outraged lawyers and courts in the countries where the data was stored. The fact that American appeals courts do not have a uniform approach to such trial court actions and the larger data-control and privacy issues only aggravates the cross-border production and cooperation problems.

A suggestion to the Team: Before even negotiating a cross-border contract, check the Sedona Conference® website for current information on international e-discovery, cross-border data transfer and data protection laws, and review the information available at its associated seminars and papers. The Sedona Conference® International Cooperation Principles provides specific guidelines for dealing with international e-discovery issues. Also read its recent policy papers on best practices in international e-discovery. When you do, remember that international best practices do not get you a pass to ignore local law. Nevertheless, international best practices will still get you a long way. Check our Resources Appendix for the link.

A SEPARATE ISSUE: COMPANY OPERATIONS ACROSS INTERNATIONAL BORDERS

We have been discussing the situation where a company in the United States does business with a company or government outside the United States. There is another equally complex situation—the multinational corporation.

These are instances where operating units in different countries are effectively controlled from one country, or where a single division of a company or organization operates across borders, only separating their operations for accounting purposes. But data and systems are commingled in one or multiple servers, providing information to all parts of the entity. In such cases, the separation of data between business units in different countries can create unique problems in the collection process. In such cases, the International Team's forensic consultant needs the assistance of not only IT and legal Team members, but also the Team's accounting members, to separate and preserve the evidence necessary for the case while protecting the content that is not relevant to the issues in dispute.

In this situation, conflicts in the data privacy laws of each country may require special handling and segregation of data from each side of the border, avoiding data movement across the line. This is a very different challenge for the International Team, since the company may be a "citizen" of both countries and subject to local punishment for decisions dictated from a distance.

MULTINATIONAL CORPORATIONS—MULTIPLE COMPLEXITIES

Multinational corporate structural issues are far above our pay grade, but the basic questions about holding, preserving, and producing electronic evidence remain the same.

In short, a company's tax or other structural decisions can change the litigation structure for a company with which you do business, or for your own company. It is always wise to check out your proposed business partner's international structure at the getting-to-know-you phase rather than when the deal has gone bad and your partner is not the corporate citizen you thought it was.

Meshing the requirements of different national laws for two different multi-nationals (even little ones) can be a complex task. As with American corporations, the location of an international company's corporate headquarters may or may not be indicative of the corporate law governing the company. And it never hurts to recheck the facts from time to time—tax structures change and so do corporate structures, and applicable e-discovery laws.

And obviously, laws and best practices change—concerning e-discovery legal practices well as computer forensics. In e-discovery as in all other areas of ESI handling, your goal is always "no surprises."

INTERNATIONAL ESI ISSUES—A FEW STATUS NOTES

Evidence Handling Issues in the Courtroom

Lawyers who have courtroom experience with cases that have an international component are aware of the requirement that a business document from another country needs special handling in order to be "evidence". This may include a requirement to have a document (including an electronic document) certified by a representative of the other country as being what you claim it is. Asking an American judge to take "judicial notice" of a provision in another country's laws means offering an English-language certified translation along with a certified copy of the original, and asking the court to accept that document as evidence of the law of the other country.

By the same token, listen to the International Team's "visiting" lawyers when they advise you about e-discovery provisions in the local laws of your partner's country. To obtain judicial cooperation from a local court for e-discovery, you may (as in Argentina, merely for example) be required to provide a copy of any supporting document, such as your contract, in the local language. Your demand that the contract be negotiated in English may come back to haunt you. Just a reminder—no surprises.

Cross-Border Forensic Practices

Computer forensics practices in another country face the same procedural challenges as documentary evidence, to say nothing of the communications challenges of translating technical forensic concepts from one language to another.

Only in 2013 did the United States Department of Justice join with the National Institute of Standards and Technology (Dept. of Commerce) to begin the task of defining specific forensic practices in the United States, through the National Commission on Forensic Science. The National Commission on

Forensic Science has begun developing standards for defining scientifically reliable guidelines for various forensic procedures, and for designing appropriate professional certifications for forensic service providers. This includes forensic collection and analysis of digital evidence.

It goes without saying that if computer forensics is not standardized within the United States, it is not standardized across the globe. As a result, any expectation by the International Team that digital evidence will be collected in a specific way in another country is an exercise in elevating stress. It is important to have a computer forensics consultant with good connections to the international professional organizations for highest-quality forensic practices. This prevents the ugly moment when your expert witness attempts to explain why digital evidence was handled badly during collection by your International Team, and is thus open to question.

Don't Forget the Economics of Preservation

The International Team's paranoia level should not in any way reflect the number of miles from your office to the location of data in another country. This is just a gentle nudge in the direction of holding onto the concepts of proportionality and cooperation. It is part of the Team's job to keep the economics of preservation and production on the table as the process proceeds.

ISO E-DISCOVERY STANDARDS ARE NOW IN DEVELOPMENT—STAY TUNED

We briefly introduced the work being done by the International Organization for Standardization (ISO), an international non-governmental organization, in connection with using the Appendix to ISO/IEC 27050-3 as a way to identify key players and the kinds of data you should be looking for and holding. We want to complete that introduction.

INCITS

ISO and the International Electrotechnical Commission (IEC) are the joint international coordinators (joint technical committee, JTC) for detailed sets of best practices, for use in every country, in computer system security and electronic data discovery, through Information Technology, Subcommittee (SC) 27. The U.S. member of ISO in this effort is the American National Standards Institute (ANSI), a division of the U.S. Department of Commerce.

For the purpose of the e-discovery and computer security international standards development, the International Committee for Information Technology Standards (INCITS) is the American technical advisory group. INCITS is open to any individual or group that wants to participate in the technical development work on these standards as part of SC27.

Among the groups that have already provided significant materials to ISO/IEC through INCITS are the Seventh Circuit Pilot Program, the New York Bar Association, the American Bar Association's Section of Science and Technology through its Electronic Discovery and Digital Evidence (EDDE) Committee, and the Department of Justice (about which we just spoke in connection with its development of forensic standards).

E-Discovery Standards Issued and In Progress

As of late 2015, the following e-discovery and digital forensics standards have been issued, within the Information Technology—Security Techniques category:

27037: guidelines for identification, collection, acquisition and preservation of digital evidence (2012):

27038: specification for digital redaction (2014);

27040: storage security (2014);

27042: guidelines for the analysis and interpretation of digital evidence (2015);

27043: incident investigation principles and processes (2015).

The following standards are in progress, to complete the suite of digital forensics standards:

27041: guidelines on assuring suitability and adequacy of incident investigative methods;

27044: guidelines for Security Information and Event Management (SEIM);

27050-1: overview and concepts—e-discovery terms, concepts and processes overview;

27050-2: guidance for governance and management of electronic discovery (including information security risks);

27050-3: code of practice for electronic discovery (6 main steps of e-discovery: identification, preservation, collection, processing, review, and production); and

27050-4: ICT readiness for electronic discovery (guidance on technology—forensic tools and systems and related processes).

These international standards will be best practices for both legal and computer forensic members of the International Team. They will not have the force of law anywhere, but are an excellent guide to the best way to meet the demands of both sides in whichever form of dispute resolution you will face if there is a triggering event in your cross-border business dealings.

It is clearly in your International Team's interests to monitor the development of local law as well as international standards on electronic discovery. Our

Resources Appendix is only a place to start in developing your own go-to list, based on your own organization's needs and experiences.

THE TRIGGERING EVENT—YOUR INTERNATIONAL TEAM IS READY

Sometimes it's just a bilingual-plus-technical miscommunication, and it gets sorted out. Sometimes no one on either side is quite sure what's happening, but it doesn't sound good. Still, everyone puts their skills to work and it gets handled. Sometimes the project has really run off the road into the ditch, and threatens to burst into flames. You know it when you see it—a triggering event.

We are assuming, by the way, that everyone is on the same page with us about events that threaten the safety of anyone involved with the project. This goes for cross-border events as well as events here at home. People come first, always. But if it is possible for tech and/or management personnel to grab the back-up external hard drives on the way, safely, out the door, that is a great help in sorting things out later. (We recollect with gratitude an office manager who stopped to grab the master back-up drives on the way out the door in the smoke and confusion of an office building fire, thus literally saving the firm.) Also, we find ourselves having to remind perfectly smart people not to stop and take cell-phone photographs while fleeing from a life-threatening situation. Perhaps that is a separate training issue—such situations happen everywhere, and are far above your authors' pay-grade. We're just about holding onto the evidence without anyone getting killed.

The Team Members Are Identified and Ready: Communication

As with your regular Incident Response Team, the members of your International Team need to be ready before there is a reason to act. They will already be familiar with each other from their contacts during the preparation and negotiation of the deal, and already know they will be called on if-and-when. The International Team leader has the contact information for all the members, both here and there. (And importantly, all the Team members know what time it is at the other members' locations, if time zones are involved.)

The Team's structure is the same, but there are more seats at the virtual table. In addition to the regular litigation-hold group here, you will have your cross-border legal and forensic consultants (who are, presumably, not on-site at the project), plus your project's on-site management liaison and technical advisor (all participating remotely from their various locations, of course).

These additions to the Team should already be trained to recognize and react to the triggering event, so they are not left standing around wondering what to do. When time zones as well as technical issues are part of the problem, be sure your entire Team has communicated together ahead of time. Each member should know how to communicate to the Team as a triggering event develops, to be sure that decisions are being made based on reliable, confirmed information about the current status of the situation.

Assessing the Skills Your Team Already Has—Don't Assume

From the digital evidence preservation perspective, you need to be ready to preserve digital evidence (including email) at your U.S. location, as well as preserving digital evidence on-site to the extent possible.

A thoughtful training session as the project is being finalized by management can minimize the cross-border confusion and time lag in getting the litigation hold into action and digital evidence secured for analysis. During this training session the Team has the leisure to identify additional technical and forensic skills the Team will need both at the home office as well as on-site. That, of course, applies to e-discovery legal-issues identification as well.

This is also the time to discover and iron out the unexpected knowledge and communication gaps on the parts of the Team members (not the least of which may be language issues).

There also needs to be technical communication about the exact forms of forensic computer techniques to be used during the litigation hold. Although the basic conversation will be between the IT and forensic consultants at home and the cross-border forensic consultant, the rest of the Team needs to know if things may be handled or reported differently than in a regular litigation hold procedure at home. As always, no surprises.

If there needs to be a special focused litigation-hold training for a designated on-site representative (and alternate), during a triggering event is not the ideal time to do it.

A training session is also an ideal time for the "home" members of the Team to receive a briefing on cultural and historical/political issues which may make activities occur in unexpected ways on-site during and after a triggering event. Your goal, as well as ours—no surprises.

SHARING TEAM LEADERSHIP CROSS-BORDER— A GREAT IDEA

You already know this—the International Team leader cannot be in two places at once. Shared leadership (with shared leadership training on cross-border issues) is the right answer. A triggering event at home demands shared leadership, shifting back and forth between legal and IT skills as the litigation hold process develops. In the same way, the leadership will need to shift between here and there with a cross-border triggering event, depending on how the triggering event itself progresses.

Autonomy for the on-site Team members can make a litigation hold situation work, especially if time-zone issues restrict the period during which it is "business hours" at both ends. Making the various transitions happen smoothly depends on good Team training as well as good Team communication.

To our International Team, *bonne chance et bon voyage*! (Good luck, and have a great trip!)

Conclusion

We invite you to set this handbook aside and consider your organization from a teamwork perspective.

When the next triggering event happens, what skill areas will be needed to handle the litigation hold? Do you have adequately skilled back-up personnel for each Team member? Do your legal department and outside litigation firm have the up-to-date skills to handle e-discovery? Where do you find an experienced, certified forensic consultant to provide the missing skills? How fast can you turn a group of your employees into a Team?

If we have given you the impression that the Team will be a room full of people, please forgive us. There will probably be one or two occasions (an initial meet-and-greet and a teamwork training session) when you will need the entire crowd, including your forensic consultant, in one place at one time. The rest of the time, it will be all about effective communication between people with different technical vocabularies sitting at different physical locations.

The core Team members—legal, IT, and management—need not be the heads of their respective work groups. You just need a person from each group who can pass the word back to that group for action as the situation progresses. Communication within the Team, and from the Team members outward to their groups and to the Team's resource members, is the goal: monitoring the identification of triggering event details and coordinating the data preservation process when the hold notice is distributed, being sure that what occurs is evidence preservation rather than just activity.

Resource members of the Team such as the Human Resources, Risk Management, Accounting, and similar members will just need to know the Team's big picture, so each of them will be ready to respond to specific queries, with the occasional direct participation in a group communication.

The ongoing structural demands on the Team, like nearly every element of the teamwork approach, depend completely on the size and complexity of your organization and the size and complexity of the triggering event.

The organization of the Team includes identifying individuals (regardless of their job titles) who have the skills the Team needs at various points in the process of responding to the event and efficiently collecting, preserving, analyzing, and delivering your electronically stored data, and supporting the litigation team in the event of a lawsuit.

Proper forensic handling of data is a fast-growing field. The 2015 amendments to the Federal Rules of Civil Procedure will affect how lawyers handle evidence, both in theory and in practice. Some of our suggestions may be "old news" in the near future, but this book is intended to lead you to current best practices that are appropriate for your organization's specific needs.

We hope this handbook provides tips for making the litigation hold a less traumatic event for your entire organization. Most of all, we hope your Team can use this handbook to ensure that your organization's name never appears in the same sentence with the words "sanctioned for evidence destruction." Remember, when things happen, Hold It.

Resource Appendix

This handbook is not an academic research publication. The authors have relied on their own decades of on-the-ground experience for most of the information contained here.

This is a work of enterprise education, intended for the in-house team conducting data preservation, for use in litigation under the Federal Rules of Civil Procedure. The resources listed below are meant to assist you in updating the information in this book with sources of practical information suitable for your own organization about the fast-developing field of electronic evidence handling.

Please note that some of our favorite blogs are associated with law firms and/or commercial companies (such as e-discovery-related software developers, etc.). Our experience with the blogs we have listed here is that they maintain e-discovery news and commentary services separate from their sales operations. We consider them, as of the time we used them in 2012–2015, reliable and independent sources of information. Be sure to check the independent status of any online source of e-discovery news. And, of course, keep an eye out for new blogs about e-discovery issues.

GENERAL RESOURCES

Publications

Federal Rules of Civil Procedure (and other federal laws, rules, and regulations): http://www.law.cornell.edu

Scheindlin, Capra and the Sedona Conference, Electronic Discovery and Digital Evidence, Cases and Materials, 3rd ed. 2015 (West Academic).

Organizations

Sedona Conference®, especially Working Group 1 (ongoing series of best-practices papers and conferences on United States and international e-discovery): https://thesedonaconference.org

American Bar Association, Section of Science and Technology, Electronic Discovery and Digital Evidence Committee (which publishes an excellent online journal, accessible to all): http://apps.americanbar.org/dch/committee.cfm?com=ST203001; for the Section: http://www.americanbar.org/groups/science_technology.html

Federal Judicial Center, Educational Programs and Materials: http://www.fjc.gov

Institute for the Advancement of the American Legal System (IAALS), University of Denver: http://iaals.du.edu

University of Houston-Clear Lake, CyberSecurity Institute: http://www.uhcl.edu/CyberSecurityInstitute

CHAPTER 1

Publications
Black's Law Dictionary, 10th Ed., 2014 (Thomson West)

Oxford English Dictionary, compact ed., 1991 (Oxford Univ. Press)

CHAPTER 2

Publications
Moore's Federal Practice (Matthew Bender, 3rd ed., 2015)

Organizations
Judicial Conference of the United States, Advisory Committee on Civil Rules: http://www.uscourts.gov/rules-policies/current-rules-practice-procedure

Blogs
Ediscovery: www.ediscovery.com/pulse (case summaries/commentaries), Kroll on Track e-discovery software company

Ediscoverylaw: http://www.ediscoverylaw.com (cases summaries/commentaries), K&L Gates law firm

In-House Counsel: http://abovethelaw.com/in-house-counsel/ (Breaking Media, Inc.)

CHAPTER 3

Organizations
FBI Cyber Action Team: FBI News Bulletin 3/6/15 https://www.fbi.gov/news/stories/2015/march/the-cyber-action-team/the-cyber-action-team

Infragard: https://www.infragard.org (FBI/private sector partnership)

CHAPTER 4

Blogs

Legaltech News: http://www.legaltechnews.com (ALM Media Properties, LLC)

CHAPTER 5

Blogs

Inhouse: http://www.inhouseblog.com (Law Department Solutions, LLC)

CHAPTER 6

Organizations

Digital Forensics Certification Board (DFCP): http://www.dfcb.org

International Information System Security Certification Consortium, Inc. $(ISC)^2$ (CCFP): https://www.isc2.org

National Commission on Forensic Science: http://www.justice.gov/ncfs

CHAPTER 8

Blogs

Exterro, Inc., case-law news: http://www.exterro.com/blog/topics/case-law-news/ (Exterro is an e-discovery and information governance software firm.)

Above the Law: http://abovethelaw.com/technology (Breaking Media, Inc.) (case news and comments, from the lawyer perspective, including technology issues)

CHAPTER 9

Publications

Here are two completely random items from local free "newspapers" in Albuquerque, merely as a sample of the level of information available to the general public. There are similar articles in publications around the country.

From "Alibi" free weekly newspaper, in the "Straight Dope: Advice from the Abyss" column by Chicago writer Cecil Adams, an article entitled "How Safe Is the Cloud?" Upshot: not very. From "Albuquerque Free Press" free weekly newspaper (May 6, 2015), "Big Data and Machine Learning Spell the End of Privacy," an article by Victor Wallace Hughes, Jr., identified as an officer in a big-data analysis start-up in Houston. It includes comments about not only Big Data, but also the Internet of Things.

We suggest that it is worth your while to monitor the level of information being presented to the community at large, as a measure of the general level of technological competence you may assume in witnesses and jurors (or not).

CHAPTER 10

Publications
Forbes magazine (Aug. 27, 2012, etc.): http://www.forbes.com/search/?q=predictive+coding

Organizations
International Organization for Standardization/International Electrotechnical Commission (ISO/IEC): http://www.iso.org

Association of Corporate Counsel, Resource Library: http://www.acc.com

Blogs
Electronic Discovery Best Practices: http://www.edbp.com (attorney Ralph Losey)

CHAPTER 11

Organizations
Seventh Circuit Electronic Discovery Pilot Program: www.discoverypilot.com

Blogs
Michael P. Carbone, attorney-mediator: http://mpcdisputeresolution.com

CHAPTER 12

Publications
Economist magazine (civil vs. common law): http://www.economist.com/blogs/economist-explains/2013/07/economist-explains-10

University of California, Berkeley, School of Law (Boalt Hall) Library (The Robbins Collection): https://www.law.berkeley.edu/library/robbins/CommonLawCivilLawTraditions.html

Best Practices in E-Discovery (New York Bar Association)

Recommendations for ESI Discovery Production in Federal Criminal Cases (US Department of Justice)

Office of the Privacy Commissioner of Canada: Privacy Handbook for Lawyers: https://www.priv.gc.ca/leg_c/guide_e.asp

Canadian Privacy Commission: Privacy Toolkit—A Guide for Businesses and Organizations: https://www.priv.gc.ca/index_e.asp

Japan privacy law: http://www.loc.gov/law/help/online-privacy-law/japan.php (US Library of Congress)

Organizations

Sedona Conference®, International Programs: https://thesedonaconference.org/conferences/intl

International Organization for Standardization / International Electrotechnical Commission (ISO/IEC): http://www.iso.org

American National Standards Institute (ANSI): http://www.ansi.org

International Chamber of Commerce, Paris: www.iccwbo.org

World Bank: http://ppp.worldbank.org/public-private-partnership/legislation-regulation/framework-assessment/legal-systems/common-vs-civil-law

European Union, General Data Protection Regulation: http://ec.europa.eu/justice/newsroom/data-protection/news/130206_en.htm

European Union Council: status on General Data Protection Regulation status: http://data.consilium.europa.eu/doc/document/ST-9565-2015-INIT/en/pdf

European Union: Binding Corporate Rules (data protection): http://ec.europa.eu/justice/data-protection/document/international-transfers/binding-corporate-rules/index_en.htm

Practicing Law Institute, International Employment Law 2015, Employee Personal Data—Cross-Border Data Privacy Challenges: http://www.pli.edu/Content/OnDemand/International_Employment_Law_2015/_/N-4nZ1z129kb?No=50&ID=225498

Blogs

Corporate Counsel: http://www.corpcounsel.com (ALM Media Properties, LLC.)

Mexico Privacy Law

http://privacylaw.proskauer.com/2010/05/articles/international/mexico-passes-sweeping-new-law-on-data-protection/

http://www.infolawgroup.com/2010/07/articles/privacy-law/mexicos-new-data-protection-law/

http://www.mondaq.com/x/184978/data+protection/Mexico+Issues+Personal+Data+Protection+Rules

China Privacy Law

https://www.huntonprivacyblog.com/tag/china/

http://privacylaw.proskauer.com/2013/02/articles/online-privacy/china-introduces-new-data-privacy-law/

Subject Index

Printed in the United States
by 500 ......

Printed in the United States
By Bookmasters